Behind You, Dad

Behind You, Dad

Finding your feet in a new land

Maxwell Mkoki

Behind You, Dad
Published by Maxwell Mkoki
with Rampart Publishing
(an imprint of Castle Publishing Ltd)
New Zealand

maxwellmkoki@gmail.com

© 2023 Maxwell Mkoki

ISBN 978-0-473-69629-0 (Softcover)
ISBN 978-0-473-69630-6 (ePUB)
ISBN 978-0-473-69631-3 (Kindle)

Editing:
Madison Hamill

Production & Typesetting:
Andrew Killick

Cover Design:
Paul Smith

Cover Artwork:
Joyce Lai

ALL RIGHTS RESERVED

No part of this publication may be reproduced,
stored in a retrieval system, or transmitted
in any form or by any means, electronic, mechanical,
photocopying, recording or otherwise,
without prior written permission from the author.

Contents

Acknowledgements	7
Preface: Parents Like Me	9
1. Expectation	13
2. Enroute	29
3. Life Overseas	39
4. Honeymoon Period	53
5. One O'clock Meetings	93
6. Baton Passing	95
7. Best in Class	103
8. Self-Meeting	125
9. Son-Dad Wish List	129
10. Mind Reader	139
11. Post Announcement Mood	169
12. Soulmate	179
13. Let It Flow	191
14. Polish Your Diamond	201
15. Flying Under the Radar and Fear	207
16. Leader by Leading	227
17. Mission Final Days	237
18. My Brother's Keeper	243
19. Sleeping in My Bed	253
20. Your Path	263
Bibliography	279

Acknowledgements

Who do you start thanking in your life other than the two people who brought you into this world? To my mum, Monica, God bless her soul who guided me from birth to the person I am today; thank you. To my dad, Walter, for the freedom you gave me to choose my path while watching from a distance. Thank you, Mavedzenge. To all my siblings who graduated from the school of house number 920 Mbaravasi Place—Coster, Onias, Conrade, Tsitsi, Colleta, Enet, and brother Victor. Thank you for your presence and guidance. I learned much from all my extended family, uncles, aunts, and cousins during our shared moments. Thank you.

My biggest fear is naming names and forgetting someone who should be on this list. To all with whom I shared a desk, a study room, a prayer room, a meditation room, a changing room, a workbench, a workplace, tools, and premises, in Zimbabwe, Italy, South Africa, New Zealand, Australia, and the USA, your presence in my life in those moments contributed immeasurably to this book; thank you.

To Gary O'Neill, you inspired and encouraged me to write events down for my son; thank you. I did it! To my editor, Madison Hamill, with your expert guidance, the project came to fruition; thank you. To Joyce Lai, I don't know how you managed to do the painting in two nights for my birthday present while capturing the book's essence, all as a surprise gift. The title was born out of the painting. Thank you. To Andrew Killick and the team at Castle Publishing Services, thank you for turning my manuscript into a gem.

To Vongaishe, thank you for our shared path, my growth, and for our son Junior. To my son Maxwell Junior, thanks for choosing us to be your parents. I am blessed to have you in my life. Our discussions became the book.

Finally, I express my gratitude to everyone who at some point was in front of me; you were all my teachers. You served your purpose in the lessons I needed to learn. Thank you, ngā mihi nui, ngiyabonga, ndinotenda.

Preface

Parents Like Me

As you grow up, you become aware of your environment, which forms part of your being—the friendly and the hostile. You notice the house you live in, the furniture, the electrical gadgets, the clothes you wear and the mode of transport. However, if it weren't for the disparities between the haves and have-nots in your community, you wouldn't notice any difference or inequality. Of course, it is ideal not to have such comparisons, but it is how humanity views the world.

Whether they come from a wealthy family or not, 'royal' or 'commoner', kids develop life-long wishes; in most cases, the dream is to improve the life they are experiencing. That wish, however, can quickly fade into obscurity if it is not nurtured.

Vice versa, most parents want their kids to have a good life, just a good life. Depending on the parents' level of abundance, the wish is for the kids to achieve more than the parents have. The innate longing in humanity is always to provide for children, and create a better world for the generations to come.

Globalisation has transformed the world from many disparate communities into something that is more interconnected. Developed countries offer better lifestyles and opportunities to people who have skills that are in short supply. Parents who dream of providing better lives for their kids get attracted to these countries…

This book is about parents, like me, who travelled thousands of kilometres and left everything behind to start a new life for themselves and their families. Their dreams, aspirations and faith that everything would work out in their favour carried most of them to places far away from their countries of birth. Most migrants I converse with, wherever they are, remember with fondness how they got their passports back from immigration offices with a work or permanent visa stamped. Excitement, a sense of achievement, the visualisation of a dream coming true, celebration and anxiety are common in their descriptions of this experience.

Before deciding which country to emigrate to, these parents researched what lifestyle that country of choice offered—the education system, health facilities, housing affordability and business opportunities. They also would have researched race relations and equality, equal employment opportunities, religious acceptability and tolerance, gender equality and human rights. Now that climate change and the environment are topical issues, some migrants are even looking at that. Usually, an assessment of the above is a good barometer of the new life.

Having done the research and secured a job or had a visa stamped on the passport, it is still natural to have feelings of doubt, fear and anxiety, as they don't know what awaits them in physical form. However, for most of these emigrants, the passion, the burning desire, the fact that they have left everything behind will urge them to keep going and focus on the objective: transforming their family lifestyle. Many emigrants are young families with no kids or young kids. When they land in the new land, the promised land, the kids have not experienced much in their country of birth. The new home to them becomes normality. The culture that seems unique and novel to the parents is not to the kids. The new culture becomes a challenge to the family as it settles, with parents wanting to pass on the cultural values they know but which conflict with the cultural influences that their kids are now exposed to in the new place. They get torn between the push to assimilate and the inclination to preserve their own culture in a new society.

Over the years, I have had discussions with my son about most of the challenges that immigrants face. These are related to employment, cost of living, language and communication, racism and discrimination, housing and accommodation, community support and government support. The 'how'—retaining helpful information, accessing advice and knowing where to get information to overcome these challenges—is the nexus to solutions. As we have these discussions, we do challenge our thinking. After having one of these talks with my son, I considered compiling and sharing my experiences, so that he or anyone who requires such advice on transitioning to a new country, or integrating into a new workplace, a new school or a new relationship, could access it through this book. The book provides steps and guidelines based on knowledge, observation and experience.

We human beings are constantly changing, and as we do, we face new challenges in our families, workplaces, schools and relationships. Yesterday's challenge might not require a solution from yesterday. The universe is constantly evolving at such a rate that your brain is not the same now as it was when you started reading this passage. For example, even though 'respect' remains respect as per its definition, the practice and value of 'respect' changes based on country, region or society. These subtle differences need perusal and to be challenged or accepted depending on which culture is dominant—the new culture versus the family's foundation culture. Several communities have established schools and cultural institutions to preserve their values and traditions when they relocate. I have nothing but respect for these communities. But immigrants from countries without cultural centres or family support face challenges and grope more in the dark for solutions than anyone else. The tribes or ethnic groups already fractured in their home countries struggle to form culture centres or groups that foster their home values when they migrate. Still, they need these resources to overcome the challenges of culture shock.

What follows is the result of my own experiences and explorations, and the gathered wisdom of others, presented as a series of conversations with my son. I hope this book helps and supports you in your own journey into new lands and unknown territories filled with possibility.

Go well, *Mwari anokutarisirai*.
Maxwell

Chapter 1

Expectation

So what were your expectations, Dad, before you decided to move us over here to Auckland? My son asked.

Junior, my situation was not different from many people who leave their countries of origin.

I paused, taking a sip of the ginger, lemon, and apple cider mix drink I usually have as my relaxing drink, thinking how best to answer him. I had been sitting with these thoughts for a while and always wanted to share the past with him. I answered: You see, the lifestyle your mum and I grew up experiencing quickly deteriorated. The education system was crumbling and getting worse before our eyes. Teachers were not getting their salaries on time, and inflation was skyrocketing daily. The teachers' motivation to give quality education was thinning day by day. Furniture in most public schools was not getting replaced, and textbooks and even sporting facilities were neglected and dilapidating. The money required to maintain them was not coming in. Parents were struggling to buy food or pay rent, mortgage and school fees. Such was the life of the common people, and such is the struggle in developing nations. You were one year old then, and I could see the economy was not improving.

Government ministers and leaders focused on enriching themselves, not the livelihood of the nation they promised to improve, and they achieved this through corrupt practices; they sent their kids overseas to developed countries with better education facilities and systems. They even flew overseas for medical reviews, I added. You see, before the corrupt, undemocratic government took over, the previous one focused on developing the country for future generations. They developed everything to world standard. People emigrating en-masse from our country to seek better lives in foreign lands was unheard of.

It took me a year to reach my decision. You had turned two when I finally said, this is it. I must make a move. I remember the date well, Son, because it was after my payday, which came on the fifteenth of every month. Pay dates were prone to changes depending on monthly company transactions. Your mum and I agreed that the fifteenth of October, after getting paid, would be the day I make a move. You see, the money we jointly earned had been eroded by inflation and shrunk so that our savings were nothing but a figure with a string of zeros—no value within or outside the country's borders. The plan was to move to a neighbouring country with a better economy, work there for a while, and use the country as the springboard to come overseas. The neighbouring country had brewing issues, but it gave us better hope and opportunities than our country.

So why were you confident that your plan would work, Dad? Junior asked.

Junior, let me have another sip of my health drink. It boosts the immune system. At least there is an end in sight to this pandemic. We didn't have that for the economic pandemic in our country, Son.

I sipped and stared at the contents of the drink that helps me wade off many winter viruses, then continued.

You see, as you develop plans to migrate, there are fears that you need to face. These fears would stop many people from achieving their dreams, whether it's emigrating, changing jobs, entering a new relationship or even starting a new course at university like you. These fears do have a habit of cropping up uninvited.

Knowing your fears gives you a better armour to deal with them when they rear their ugly heads. Do you know what I mean by the ugly head of fear? Junior shook his head. Indecision, procrastination, fear of criticism, doubt, I listed, counting them off with my fingers.

> The ugly heads of fear:
> – Indecision
> – Procrastination
> – Fear of criticism
> – Doubt

You see, Son. I swallowed. I had a strong desire to relocate for a long time. Long before you were born. But I remained hopeful that our country's prospects would improve. My dissatisfaction and aggravation grew as things degenerated. One of my close friends, Kenny, had emigrated three years earlier, though, for me, it had been a case of *go, don't go, go, don't go*. But with you coming into our lives, I finally said, *If you want Junior to have a better life, you better go now*. It was a joint decision with your mum, I said, rewinding the past.

Earlier, I had many reasons for not taking the plunge. The company I worked for had good forecasts in the three years preceding the decision. The market was good, and the company was the sole manufacturer of the product that we were making. Growth opportunities were huge. But the central governments hindered whatever progress most companies were making. Coupled with high taxation and foreign currency shortages, companies struggled to make any meaningful progress, I explained. So, my job was one excuse; leaving behind familiar neighbourhoods, family members and friends was another excuse for not relocating.

Even though I could foresee the country was going into a continuous negative spiral, I had close friends and family who always talked me out by pointing to some bright future somewhere on the horizon. I think I tried to walk to the horizon, but with every step I took towards it, it also moved a step back; it became unreachable, and eventually I ran out of energy; I got tired and stopped. But yes, the fear of criticism delayed my decision. Doubt always crept in after discussions with friends and family about the pros and cons of migrating, I said, justifying my delay.

Was it like peer pressure you always warn me against, Dad? Junior asked.

I thought about this for a moment and responded. Peer pressure is when all your friends encourage you to change your behaviours and attitude to match theirs, Son; in this case, I was split in-between. I had friends who had left the country and friends still in the country, so the choice was mine and mine alone. Fear in me was the pressure, I clarified.

Dad... Junior began to ask another question.

Hold on, one moment, Son, let me get my salted peanuts, you know, my favourite snacks I always keep in the pantry. They go along well with this ginger, lemon, apple cider concoction.

Oh, Dad. You and your nuts... Junior laughed.

Yes, my nuts and I are close buddies... why are you laughing? I responded, laughing as well.

Do you regret that it took you a while to decide to move? he asked.

Yes and no, Son, I answered. Yes, in the sense that maybe it would have given me more time to be in this beautiful country I finally chose, and no, because if we had moved sooner you wouldn't have been born. Your mum and I were not married then.

We both laughed, then Junior quickly continued, So the delay and our journeys could have been preplanned by some external force, the All, the source, or his planning committee? he asked.

I had not thought of it that way, Son, I answered, which reminds me, you know one thing these billionaires have in common? I paused, thinking of how the world's wealth is growing each day and how so much wealth can be found with a few individuals. Going on: There are so many of them now that you can find them in most countries with 'smart' people. Most of them tend to reach their decisions quickly when given all the facts and take ages to change them if they ever change. A good example is a fellow called Henry Ford.

You mean of Ford cars, Dad? Junior chipped in.

Yes, Son, I answered. He is long gone but respected for how he made decisions back then. He made quick decisions and took ages to change them, like what he did on the Ford T model, which went into production for ten years in one colour, black. But, of course, a lot has changed; companies now need to be agile or they'll quickly sink—the competition is challenging and fast-paced. A new breed of thinkers and innovators like Elon Musk have upended old strategies.

Why quick decision-making, Dad? Junior queried. How does that relate to their billion-dollar wealth you mentioned? You also used the words 'smart people'. Does that mean anyone without a billion dollars in their name is not smart? You always say we should not compare ourselves with others, but—

I stopped Junior in his track. Hold on, Son, I know where this is going; I am going to try to answer all your questions to the point that you understand and you can do further checking on your own; that's what you do in school and uni, right?

I carried on. These guys decide so quickly based on their confidence in their support team; they put a lot of effort into surrounding themselves with intelligent subject matter experts. They headhunt the best people to be part of their team. They know that a quick decision-making strategy would be futile without these necessary brains, and competitors would continually outpace them. So now you see, Son, why it's essential to have intelligent people in your team.

I get your point, Junior concurred, nodding.

Going back to how we ended up in this country... sorry, Son, I easily get distracted; it comes with old age, I said, grinning ear to ear.

But you are not old yet, Dad. You are just middle-aged, whatever that means, Junior quipped.

Yes, Son, I know, I said, but it is halfway to the century mark, and a while back, that age was the life expectancy of humans and yes, I am aging well, thanks for reminding me, I said, stroking my ego.

There you go again, Dad, but you always say we should be humble.

I laughed. Just joking, Son; you know how I joke when I am with you, I wouldn't say that outside this conversation. Anyway, it's important to have good friends whom you can rely on, and they on you.

It was important that I tell Junior this, because my grandkids would want to know in the future how the journey started for us to end up on these shores. We learn through history, whether it's through books, teachers or oral history. Society's past failures and successes guide future generations. I went on: In my organisation back in our country, I collaborated with overseas consultants as well as regional. When our company ran into operational problems that required outside help, we engaged these consultants to help us resolve difficult production issues. The consultants would gather data before tackling the problem. I would supply the consultant with much of the information required. They relied on me to help them resolve the issues, hence becoming good friends, I said.

Good for you, Dad, Junior complimented

Smiling and eager to finish that part of the story, I carried on: I took off to my friend's country when dissatisfaction became too much to bear. I rang my friend Nick soon after landing and asked him to arrange a job because I would not return. He consulted for several organisations and had a good network of recruitment specialists. I knew he had confidence in my performance, and I did not hesitate to tell him my intentions. 'Right decision,' Nick said, 'leave everything to me.' No references and curriculum vitae were required; Nick knew my employment history and qualifications. Within a day of contacting him, I had a job and money for settling in.

I paused, taking a breather, replaying in my mind how events had panned out. It's moments like these where past events become timeless and emotions become alive again. I went on: It was after getting employed that I was asked to give my resumé for filing purposes. So, you see the importance of alliances with good friends and being good to everyone, I concluded.

Develop friendships, network with good people, Son. You can see how someone treats others, how they describe people who are different or less fortunate than them, how they respect other people outside their class if at school or outside work, and how they behave at social gatherings. How empathetic they are or how sarcastic, deceitful or likely to emotionally harm others, I advised. Junior nodded in agreement.

I continue, It reminds me of the first days we landed here. I drove around with George, who had the courtesy of showing me around. I commented to him that Auckland City was multicultural. Then, I mentioned how one ethnic group, the Asian community, was quite noticeable in some places we had visited. Coming from Africa, I didn't know what to expect, I had not looked at ethnicity statistics in my research. Then George said, 'Oh, there is quite *an awful lot of them here.*' Laughing. I thought, umm, that's not a good statement and reaction. Why would one say such a statement as 'awful' unless he despises Asian people? I also wondered about his opinion of my ethnic group as it was different from his. We did not encounter anyone who looked like me. George did not reveal what he thought about my ethnicity. Generally, he seemed to have dry descriptions of ethnic groups in his vocabulary. Well, in short, it turned out that he was not that Mr Nice Guy he was portraying himself to be. So, be careful who you incorporate into your circle of friends; you want them to uplift you and vice versa, share positive energy and not drain you with their negativity.

Junior then comments, ignoring my last tale, You were lucky to land a job within a day in a foreign country, Dad.

Yes, I concurred, then I added, I can't deny that, Son. Nevertheless, you see, there are some specific principles that you need to adhere to for luck to find you. 'Lucky' is a word that I don't remember hearing much growing up. I was not sure why it was not a popular word. But I think I know now why. See, luck does not build any road, house or car, or get people degrees, it does not make people rich, or give them a good husband or wife, or land people like me jobs. I will explain further another time, Son. We've got nothing to do this weekend anyway; let's carry on this conversation later.

The city, the country, and most parts of the world were still under lockdown as we had this conversation. New Zealand was in 'Alert Level 4' after a community case, presumed to be infected with the Delta variant of Covid-19, had been detected. With nothing much to do inside the house, people resorted to finding ways of passing the time productively; baking became a number one pastime, along with board games, Netflix watching, etcetera.

This was the ideal period to build relationships; for me, the time was perfect to pass on the events of our journey to the present moment. Making the most of the time we share with our family, friends, relatives and everyone else is what makes life worth living.

Adding stars to a gloomy painting transforms it, enlivens the viewer's mood and perception. What we perceive becomes who we are. Any event is viewable in two settings; our choice determines our happiness. The lockdown could not lock our moods unless we allowed it to.

As I stood up to go to the bathroom, I glanced out the living room window. A streak of sunshine invited me out for a stroll after completing bathroom business, but it was cloudy and a bit cold for my liking at sixteen degrees Celsius. Auckland's weather is at its most unpredictable in August. I let the invite pass as I stopped to admire the elephant-head portrait, which watches all my movements in the living room. The elephant is my family totem. Junior was on his phone as I continued past him to the passage that leads to the bathroom.

I checked the WhatsApp and Messenger messages that had pinged earlier. I checked for what to watch next on Netflix, but nothing caught my attention. I walked back to the living room, and before I sat down, Junior asked: Which are the specific principles that need to be followed, which you were talking about, Dad? I have wondered what you mean by that.

****

Lucky is a word you can use if you want to be humble about your achievements, Son, I said, smiling. On the other hand, lucky is a word used by people who want to take away others' achievements. Lucky is a blaming word for those who do not have the success recipe.

How so, Dad? Junior asked.

Simply put, you would have seen long winding queues at the corner dairy, supermarket or any shop that sells Lotto tickets when the jackpot goes up. You have accompanied me as well to the Lotto shop several times. What we will be doing is obeying the 'luck' rules. We will be busy buying ourselves spots along the motorway. You see, luck has strict rules and demands that his rules get followed. I stopped midway then added, Sorry, no, my mistake, *her* rules. I think luck is a woman like my mother; God bless her soul, wherever she looks upon us. Your grandma was strict about following her directions, or you were instantly disciplined.

I reflected on how raising children was evolving rapidly. My mum would just call you in a tone that made you self-correct if you were misbehaving as you wouldn't want Dad's brown belt on your bottom.

I continued. On the other hand, luck does not punish you. However, when it comes to Lotto gaming, you must have purchased a spot along the highway so that when she decides to reward you for being a nice person, she will stop by your location on her way to hand you your prize. Therefore, *an effort* has to be put in for you to get rewarded, I said, thinking of another example.

After the second lockdown, as you know, I had a side job. My boss, Rod, addressed the warehouse staff, thanking us for adhering to the two-metre rule, sanitising our hands and workstations and putting on face masks as soon as we entered the premises or when we took public transport. He was one of the most empathetic managers I have worked under in this country, and humble. He came down to your level when you had a one-on-one discussion. Also, I'm inclined to throw in the word 'modest'. Towards the end of his speech, he said, 'We are *lucky* as a country that we haven't had so many deaths from Covid-19.' I had to bite my tongue, and yes, I did manage to stop interrupting his speech.

What were you thinking? Junior quizzed.

I quickly explained that one had to look at the government and its health department's efforts, like continuous monitoring and improvements implemented when the system had shown cracks and gaps. To get such a low number of deaths when some parts of the world were burying thousands of people a day was a testimony of hard work and effort, not *just* luck. Luck went around the world, picking up the countries following its rules and awarding them the desired results. *Desire* is what you need, burning desire and the will to act *plus* effort to produce the results you want, Son.

You are digressing, Dad. Since I will tell your story to your grandkids, you need to keep on track with your journey, so it is easy for me to understand.

That's a good point, Son. Always focus on the task at hand in whatever you are doing. Also, it is good to have someone who can remind you that you are going off track, nudge you to keep track of your set targets, right? I said, grinning.

True, concurred Junior.

Silently, I recalled some research I'd read about thoughts. Humans are constantly getting swayed off track by many thoughts that pass through their minds; sixty to seventy thousand thoughts go through our minds per day, and if we are not in charge, we end up clasping onto the unproductive ones.

I remember with fondness the time I spent at my transit job in South Africa, I said. One of the reasons was the seamless transition into the new role. The workforce was quite friendly, and I never saw myself as a man from Zimbabwe. However, there were cultural differences; I had mentally prepared myself to settle in, and my new team's welcoming attitude made the process easy. It was quite gratifying, to say the least. Positivity is contagious, and it propels anybody to accomplish their goals. If you plant an idea in your mind with conviction and honestly believe in that idea, you will always have the assurance of a positive outcome. How that comes is not for your conscious mind to worry about.

What do you mean, Dad? You are losing me. Junior commented.

I nodded and said, You are right, Son. Let me try to break this down further, but before that, let me pass on this profound statement I got from Napoleon Hill's book, *Think and Grow Rich*. He wrote that 'whatever the mind can conceive and believe, it can achieve'. Meaning anything you set out to achieve and believe will come to fruition. If you are passionate about it to the point that every night before you go to sleep, you tell yourself that 'I've got to have that', whatever it is you have set your mind on, when you wake up in the morning, you tell yourself the same, 'I've got to have it', you will start coming up with ideas, ways, and means of achieving that goal. What stops you and me from achieving what we want in life is the limitations we set ourselves in our minds or allow others to set for us. See, I said, *allow others*. It's because it is we who give anyone permission to set that limitation on our goals, I explained.

You see... I stopped and walked to the pantry to get some salted nuts; I liked the taste of roasted groundnuts as a three- or four-year-old living with my grandma, and the affinity never left; some bits of the past never leave us.

Drinking 'concoctions' was part of my growing up as well. My grandma would pick her small hoe from the hut. She would suspend it on her shoulder with her duffel bag in hand; into the woods she went, and she would come back with all sorts of roots and leaves, put them in a pestle, and mortar mix them into a concoction. She would then put it into a cup, add water and give it to any of us who complained of any ailment. In no time, you would be as fit as a fiddle.

I resumed: Any situation you are in, if you feel someone is stopping you from achieving your goals, you have *permitted* that person to put limits on your goals. However, you also have options to remedy and reverse the situation altogether, like reporting them, confronting them or leaving the place and finding another source for growth.

> Options when someone is standing in the way of your goals:
> – Reporting the person
> – Confronting the person
> – Leaving the place
> – Finding another source for growth

I have found these four options to work for me. I am sure they can work for you, Son, if you are in a similar situation, I advised.

How do you set limitations for yourself, Dad? Junior asked.

Good question! I think your kids would be asking the same questions as you, but remember, you will need to encourage them to question anything and everything from an early age as I did with you. If no one asked questions, society would not meaningfully develop.

Through questioning and curiosity, you develop your thinking abilities and accountability, and so does the community.

When you want something, it is you who decide, and no one tells you what to like unless you accept it. You have complete control of your mind. Your mind is a faculty that no one else can have control of other than you, the owner. When you set goals, you can also seek out 'enablers'—those who can help you achieve your goals. However, even those who are helping you cannot change your dreams unless you allow them, I added.

When you were born, you came to this world with no information about your new life but only emotions to respond with. Your mum and I, the TV, teachers, friends, family, community, and everything you met, gave you bits and pieces of information and you stored it in your memory bank. Bank, yes, it is a bank. You use your memory bank the same way as your financial bank. Information gets withdrawn and handed to you whenever you need answers, and the task gets completed. Any questions that require the information you have used before get filled in accordingly. Also, all the time, you are constantly depositing information into your memory bank through your thinking. You have, however, the option to choose the information you want to use for any given task. Like the mixed currency account in your typical bank, you can say I want to use the US dollar today, or the Euro, the Pound, the Aussie dollar or the Kiwi dollar, and you will get that currency. Your mind does the same thing. That is where *control of your mind* comes in. You are the master of your mind. Your mind does not control you, regardless of your upbringing. You own how you want to act or permit someone to do it for you. I stopped to see a reaction from Junior, who then gestured for me to carry on, and I did.

Success has no limitations, but you do—only the ones you have set up for yourself or allowed others to set for you. You can remove those limitations within yourself. If you look deep down, in your memory bank, you can throw stuff out that is not required and make room for things that allow you to achieve whatever you desire. Similarly, the way you handle your standard mixed current bank account, means you can choose to remove useless currency and replace it with money that has more value and is accepted worldwide. However, your memory bank is hard and fast when removing the trash from the account. When you send mixed messages, it gets confused. Akin to saying, 'draw', when you mean 'remove'. Eventually, it becomes stubborn and keeps both the trash and good stuff. It will have picked up that you do not want to let go of it. All sorts of alibis can come up for not letting go—parents, community, neighbourhood, teachers, managers, government. But no one can stop you from achieving your dream if you have a plan.

Remember what I said earlier on about billionaires and smart people? A good example is a billionaire in Africa, called Strive Masiyiwa. He had a dream and a goal that no one could extinguish. Yes, even his government could not stop him from achieving his dream. It was not an illegal venture, but a desire to provide a life-changing service to society. With the best legal advice, he took the government to court. He was frustrated for five long years by the court system. But he remained persistent, relentless, and unwavering in his quest to get what he desired. Eventually, the court found the government wrongfully impinging on his rights as a citizen. Then the court ordered the government to grant him the mobile operating license to start his business. While waiting for the court process, he must have developed bigger dreams of going global, such that when he got the operating license, he grew his business into several countries across the globe. His strength grew out of the struggles the government subjected him to. No limitations on his dreams could stop him from achieving his goal and desire. *You have the ultimate control*, I concluded, reflecting on how the information applied to me as well. As I was saying the words, I realised that I was a work in progress; there were gaps that needed my attention. I had projects I had stopped pursuing and not seen to fruition because of competing priorities or unseen obstacles.

Chapter 2

Enroute

It took a couple of months for you and your mum to come and join me down south in Joburg and live as a family again. I constantly questioned whether the country was ideal for raising you in the waiting period. The culture was different from our own, which was a slight worry. My sister had lived in South Africa for three years before my move. She had been filling me in with all the information I needed about liveability. Being an avid follower of world news helped me keep track of statistics in areas I was interested in. I was well-versed in things like the prevalence of violent crime, the cost of education, the availability of affordable housing and even the safest parts of the city to raise a family.

I found the reality not to be very far from the reported statistics. One early morning on my way to the bus terminus, a distance of about a hundred metres, I walked past a dead body lying next to the road, and people walked past as if it was nothing unusual, and no one seemed to care. It was shocking and gruesome to me. However, in this neighbourhood, Alexandra, it was normal. Fridays and Saturdays were the high crime days. Police would come after sunrise, doing their routine drive and picking up dead bodies. My sister had warned me about her neighbourhood, where this was the norm then. She later moved to Lyndhurst, a safer suburb.

When you joined me however, we lived in a safer area, a good neighbourhood by any standard, Elspark in Germistone, east of Joburg. It was a gated community, Katarina Place, where you had to pass through a security gate to go in and out, which to me was like being a prisoner in your own home. We were like animals fenced in a zoo in our homes. That kept me thinking that this was not how I wanted to live my life each time I passed through the gate. I realised you must trade in one for another; no one has it all. To be safer, we had to live this way. A law of harmony says we adjust to our environments, like mammals in cold climates adapt to grow enough fur for them to survive the conditions. Camels adjust to desert conditions and migratory birds travel thousands of kilometres when they don't have the right conditions.

When you have a destination to reach, regardless of how good the conditions are at the port you have docked, you must continually remind yourself that the goal hasn't been born yet. Like a docked ship, necessary routine checks need to be carried out. The engine needs a good daily run to keep it in peak condition. The ship might be waiting for the cyclone or typhoon season to pass, or whatever the case. I kept asking myself the question, *Why am I here?* That question stirred my insides and stoked up the ambers within, constantly pushing me to search for opportunities in countries where I could live freely and permanently.

The fact that I was in transit did not stop me from performing to the best of my abilities at work, right to the very end. Management even asked if I could recommend any former workmates keen on crossing the border and working for the company. I had brought my work ethic, which prompted the company to search for employees like me.

No one at that workplace knew that I had plans to move overseas. It is vital not to reveal your goals except to those you know will assist. Experience and observation have taught me that when the stakes are high, it's best to let the achievement announce itself.

A football player on loan to another club does not stop performing to his best ability because he got loaned out. However, if the player has decided that he wants to be in the first team, his mother team, he will always excel, be recalled, and reclaim his position in the first team.

You might be in school or in a relationship or work situation. If you've set an initial goal and have not reached that goal, always remind yourself that the journey is still on. You need to hold that certificate, that degree, in your hands. If it is a happy relationship you want, you are still on course to your goal as long as you contribute your part of the bargain. If it is a work role, keep performing to your best. You will earn your reward. If it is business, keep innovating and give your customers what they want beyond their expectations.

> It is vital not to reveal your goals except to those you know will assist. When the stakes are high, it's best to let the achievement announce itself.

What else was reminding you of your goals, Dad? Junior asked, then added, You know you have always said that you need to write your goals down in your diary that you keep on you. You read it aloud before you sleep and when you wake up in the morning before you start your day.

Excellent recall, Son! I quipped. You are a good student; that's exactly how you keep your goals at the forefront of your thinking. Repetition will bank the information in your subconscious mind and will eventually turn that information into physical form by giving you the means to get to your end. It is best to have invincible determination, be self-driven and be emotionally involved for the results to manifest.

You will not remember that we lived a few suburbs from the airport in South Africa. We could see planes coming to land and taking off. I frequently shouted out loud to planes flying past when we took afternoon strolls. 'Please take us with you,' I would say. It was funny to you. You would laugh and giggle; you were three, your dad talking to airplanes up in the sky. Deep down, that's what I wanted to happen. You must keep the burning desire to reach your goals alive.

Here are some common steps for setting any goal, Son; I will not re-invent the wheel. Visualise the results you want to achieve. Create a SMART goal; it must be Specific—you have to specify exactly what you want to do, for example, build muscles. It must be Measurable—for example, you have to set aside days and time you do your workout or go to the gym. It must be Attainable—you have to have a nearby gym and all the equipment for your workout to happen. It must be Relevant—How will the building of the muscles change your life situation? And it must be Time-bound—Lock your goal into a specific timeframe and decide when you complete it by, like when you want your muscles to show. Write your goal down. Create an action plan. Create a timeline. Act, and re-evaluate and assess your progress.

These steps are the most used tools in project management, and they should be your tools as well. Let these be foundations for whatever goal you want to achieve. I did not have these tools or anyone to tell me the exact steps I needed to follow, but that's the detailed plan I was following. I believe the early explorers were following the same processes too: having a journey in mind, estimating how long it would take, how much food they would require, the clothing they would need, the workforce required, the common challenges and how to overcome them.

So that's what I did. I identified the countries I wanted to emigrate to, I *visualised* the life I wanted. I made sure I had the skill set

> Steps for setting a goal:
> - Visualise the results you want to achieve.
> - Create a SMART goal; It must be:
>   - Specific
>   - Measurable
>   - Attainable
>   - Relevant and
>   - Time-bound.
> - Write your GOAL down.
> - Create an ACTION plan.
> - Create a TIMELINE.
> - Act.
> - Re-evaluate and assess your progress.

that matched demand in those countries. We had no computers and smartphones for the internet in those days but had internet cafés, so I would spend an hour in the café looking for job opportunities, applying, and checking my emails online. I looked for companies in the same sector as I was. I made sure that my resumé was current. I made sure that all my referees were aware of the possibility of being contacted. This was all part of my *action plan*. I ensured that I worked for reputable companies that would be easy to reach should prospective employers cross-reference overseas. To be safe, I double-checked that all my credentials and travel papers were current.

Junior jumped in: I'm not sure if I need the last bit of information, Dad. You made the best choice for us to move to this country. I don't have plans ever to emigrate. All I have and want is in this country. My friends and childhood memories are here.

My home is here, and I don't get treated differently in school and social life, even though I look different. You know all my friends from my childhood. You know their parents too; you remember our sleepovers as kids. For now, I've no reason to think I need the information, he concluded.

You never know, Son, when information will come in handy; growing up, I never thought that I would leave my country and everything, but circumstances changed. You came along, and I couldn't envision you growing up in the deteriorating conditions I was witnessing. The chances of that ever happening here are quite minimal. Experience has taught me never to say never. Unless you are as sure as the sun that does its daily routine without fail, rising on one horizon and setting on the opposite.

Junior hesitated. You are probably right, Dad. I might need the information one day. I might marry someone who wants to experience life overseas or get a job that requires me to live overseas. I might venture into entrepreneurship, and my market would require me in another country.

Now you are thinking broad, Son, and I'm not encouraging you to move to another country at some point as the decision will be entirely yours. I'm just passing some information to you, Son, which I have acquired over the years.

Junior affirmed, You aren't doing a bad job. He laughed.

I'll repeat the story as long as you need it, if I'm still here, I quipped. I hope I won't be as grumpy as your granddad.

I bet you wouldn't say that in front of him, would you? Junior probed.

Of course, I would; I did the other day in a WhatsApp video call when the word 'grumpy' came into our conversation; I said, 'How is grumpy Walter these days?' and he went, 'Oh pretty good, how about grumpy Maxwell?'

We both laughed. Telling the story made me think. You know,

I said, he is thirteen thousand kilometres away, but the marvel of technology brings us into the same room. Technology has removed the distance between families split apart by emigrating.

Hope you still remember where you left with your story before you digressed, Junior said, nudging me back to the storyline.

Yes, Son, very well, though even when I get to a hundred and two years old, and you ask me to narrate the story, I would do it the way I am doing it now, I laughed.

Why a hundred and two, Senior? Junior quizzed.

I know I'll get to that age, Son, and I just feel I need to hit that century mark and be able to tell stories to my great, great, great grandkids. That's my wish, I said. I always liked to be surrounded by people who emit positive energy. Those who, when they talk, make you energised and uplifted, regardless of the conversation topic. The people who are like the morning sunshine you enjoy walking in, running in, gardening, whatever you like doing before the sun gets too hot. Depending on where you are, if you look hard enough, you will connect with these people if you are on the same vibe.

My routine after work was to go and check my emails for replies and job offers at the internet café. Occasionally, I'd bump into one of my good friends who also visited the café. We'd have our friendly chat before proceeding to pay for my one-hour internet browsing time. An internet café had about twenty desktop computers spaced out like a classroom. Customers paid for use at the counter and time was credited to the computer they would use.

On this day, there was one spot left. I tiptoed to the vacant computer desk. Internet cafés were library-like, quiet, everyone busy doing whatever they were doing; only the clicking of the mice and punching of the keyboards is what you would hear. I opened my mailbox and checked my favourite websites dedicated to my field. Updates of the new technology, upcoming seminars and job vacancies across the world were my favourite sections, so I browsed down the lists, and *boom*, there it was, mid-table. The job matched my training, experience and qualifications to a T. I knew it was my job, and I went 'YES!' and pumped my fist. I demonstrated this to Junior, and went on: People looked up to see the source of the sound. 'YES!' I repeated. I had my resumé on a floppy disk, which I always carried in my backpack. I hurriedly took the disk out, slotted it into the computer slot area then proceeded to apply and attach my resumé. When I got home, I told your mum excitedly that I had found the job that would take us away from this place. I kept repeating that it was *my* job and was waiting for me. She told me to calm down, for I could get disappointed. I calmed down a bit but could not wait to go back to the café the following day after work to check my inbox for the reply.

The next day became one of the slowest days ever in my work life. Such that as the clock struck four o'clock, knock-off time, I bolted out of the gate to catch a taxi to the café. I felt a dream coming true, a sense of achievement. I quickly paid for my one-hour computer browsing period. I opened my inbox, and indeed, there it was, a very promising reply, which said my application had been received and the company would proceed to check and verify my details, then get back to me.

I smiled as I noticed Junior taking mental notes. Then he asked, How did the reply make you feel?

There was no doubt in my mind, Son, that the job was mine. *How?* I had a strong feeling, an intuition. Being positive brings positive results, being negative attracts negative results and being neutral cancels it all out and leaves you in the same position. If it failed to materialise, there were lessons to be learned, I was positive, I answered.

I will keep that in mind, Junior said.

We become what we think about, I added. I told myself to wait a few days before sending a follow-up email. I did not have to wait for long. The following day the organisation emailed asking me to come overseas for an interview. The dream was coming true. Your mum could not believe what was happening. It took a couple of months for the visa application to be processed, and then I was on the plane—that aeroplane I had once wished would take me away. Sure enough, it came to take me to a place far, far away.

The interview took five working days. I also had the weekend to feel out the country and the city. I got the job and had to go back and process work-to-resident visas for you and your mum so we could start a new beginning again as a family.

Just before Christmas and within the two-year timeline that I had marked in my goal-setting, we were moving to this beautiful country we call home today. Can you say that we were lucky, Son? I would say I followed luck's rules. I did what I had to do for luck to find us. I went to the internet café to look for luck. I compiled my resumé and kept it with me so that 'luck' could call me anytime; I kept working to the best of my ability at my job, so that when 'luck' would ask for a job reference, she would get a clean connection. I did all I needed to do and waited to receive luck. I asked; I believed and accepted what got handed to me. And that's how we left the shores of Africa for these shores we are on now, Son.

Chapter 3

Life Overseas

What was starting a new life in a new country like, Dad? Junior asked. Different culture, different accent, and different standards in everything you knew?

I responded, You probably remember bits and pieces of incidents when we landed as you were four years old, turning five. I remember you recounting not long ago how we were picked up from the airport and dropped at the motel. I might go on and on about that, but what is important to remember is, expectations will not always match reality every step of the way. Anticipation has the power to change the chain of events like a forked road.

Many people take up residence or citizenship in another country because they want better opportunities for themselves and their families. Better than they had in their mother-countries. But opportunities come along with challenges that you must overcome. You need to set yourself financial rules. The rules you will abide by will depend on how you immigrated.

The important thing is to set yourself up a good foundation. Like putting aside at least ten percent of your earnings. If your net income is $1000 a week, from that point on, what should click in your mind is that you are earning $900. All your other expenditures will be based on ten percent less of your salary or wages. You need to pay yourself first before anyone else, I said.

Fair enough, yes, it makes sense, Dad, Junior concurred.

You are working, so you need that compensation for your future self. You carry on saving ten percent until you retire, that is how you build your fallback resources. Remember you are in this new country—you came all this way because you want to add to whatever you have or start afresh from the ground up. Although, this financial self-discipline applies to anyone, migrant or not, I said.

What if my expenses require more money, and the only money I have for the added expenses would be in my savings account? Junior asked. Should I reduce the amount I save, say to six or eight percent?

Do not mix up necessary expenses with wishes, Son, I answered. You can forgo desires until they can get accommodated within the budget of ninety percent income. You can ride your cravings until you have the money to buy the horse; we all have desires that our earnings cannot gratify. What is important is to live within your income.

Self-discipline is paramount if those wishes requiring your expenditure will take more than your regular budget. Or you may end up in perpetual debt. Rather be a 'slave' to your budget than a 'slave' to your bills.

I found out when I opened my bank account that the bank could allocate me a banking advisor if I required one. This was amazing news, because the next step in setting up your financial foundation is to have an expert who can give you advice on all financial matters: how to grow your money, when to grow your money, where to grow your money. Banks and financial advisors have the knowledge and expertise to help propel you to economic heights. Asset and investment advisers are equally important as well. You might need to approach them separately from your bank. It is also necessary to research their advice before you make decisions. For example, my advisor asked me to set financial goals for myself at the level of risk I could accommodate. He designed my portfolio in such a way that it incorporated all my goals.

You already have a bank account. When your income changes, you need to let your bank advisor know, and they can advise on how to adjust and maximise returns on your new income.

Don't be hesitant or procrastinate, or money will also be indecisive and procrastinate getting into your bank account. Money is shy coming to you, but poverty is brutal; hence there are no poverty advisors, only financial advisors. You need to be prompt when making financial changes that benefit and boost your income.

> Don't be hesitant or procrastinate, or money will also be indecisive and procrastinate getting into your bank account.

I know you have childhood friends. Having good friends was quite helpful again when we first got here. Friends should be valued. Your mum and I decided who we wanted to be our friends.

We told ourselves, *We are in a new country*. Just like kindergarten kids, we were learning a lot of stuff and needed family friends who were honest, not deceitful and manipulative, to help ease our settling.

But we needed them to be accepting of our differences. We did not want to be changed entirely, but we wanted friends who would help us with baby-step changes, not pressure us to buy this and that, or visit that place, eat out at this place, ask us why we were living where we were or tell us to send you to this kindy or that school. We needed people around us who could accommodate *our* needs.

We had an acquaintance who was overly keen to be with us whenever they had free time, which we found quite overbearing.

We said to ourselves that as much as we appreciated their appetite to help us settle, they were missing the point that we needed time for ourselves as well; when we subtly told them about our need to have time to ourselves, they did not take it lightly.

We also thought having a friend who could view a situation from someone else's perspective, who was non-judgmental, was worth having around, compared to someone who passes comments without regard to the effects of their words on others. Another one was loyalty. We identified acquaintances we thought were genuine and not gossiping about other people in the community; we agreed it was an attractive trait to have in a friend. Additionally, no one likes a person who is not respectful of both themself and others; this was easy for us to identify in any of our friends.

We told ourselves, this might take a while, but we would like to have friends we can trust and who can trust us too. We wanted people who shared our principles. We also identified those with kids the same age as you as prospective friends.

We looked for things like self-confidence. It is inadvisable to have a friend who is not self-confident, as they will deflate you with their comments. I once had a workmate who constantly complained about everyone and everything so that you would feel drained the longer you were around him. Such people say negative stuff about others regardless of the relationship. They're generally small-minded people.

I would also suggest surrounding yourself with those who are positive influences, intellectually or through self-development. Your friends' collective thinking processes will affect your decision-making processes in the long run. So, it is essential to have bright and intelligent friends.

You've just turned twenty, and I still worry about what you do or where you are with your friends. I am unsure if my dad worried

> How to pick your friends:
> - Accepting
> - Accommodating
> - Non-judgmental
> - Loyal
> - Respectful
> - Principled
> - Self-confident

much about me growing up. It is because I was in a familiar neighbourhood, where everyone knew everyone. We don't even know our neighbours who live two houses from us on either side here. I find that not everyone wants to know everyone here, people keep to themselves, which is not what a healthy community should be. However, we have had some good neighbours over the years in this country. The ones that were not good we never noticed.

It's important to look for friendliness in people, a smile, a good morning, a wave, stopping for a chat. These you need to reciprocate to your neighbours.

Finally, you need to break the ice yourself. Remember our neighbours, whom I rate the best neighbours we ever had here? When we bought our first home, Cathy, the wife, welcomed us with a cake. They told us they had been living in their house for more than forty years and briefed us about our new suburb's history—how good and safe the suburb was. Both Cathy and Bobby, the husband, who had been in the Second World War, had been exposed to different cultures. Bobby was a Justice of the Peace, so it was second nature to be friendly and neighbourly. Not every neighbour will welcome you with a cake like Bobby and Cathy. God bless his soul, Bobby passed on four years later, in his nineties.

When Bobby's health deteriorated, he had a bad fall in the lounge; Cathy rushed to us for help to lift and put him in a recovery position. When St John's ambulance arrived, he said, 'I'm fine. It's Cathy who is being melodramatic by calling the ambulance.' The veteran fighter was still in him. Two days later, I visited him at the hospital, and he thanked me for helping him and Cathy. 'No worries, Bobby, you are a good man,' I responded. Unfortunately, his health did not improve much, so his family decided to move him to a village to get prompt assistance. Unfortunately, he did not live long in the retirement village before passing. I went to his funeral, and the eulogies confirmed how good a person he was. We were blessed to have had a neighbour like Bobby.

Always be courteous and have a warm smile for your neighbours, Son, as they might be the first port of call when disaster falls upon you; this, I am passing on to you and the generations to come. I am not an expert in scriptures, but a verse says you shall love your neighbour as yourself, just like Bobby and Cathy did to us.

> Your neighbours might be the first port of call when disaster strikes:
> – Look for friendliness in people, a smile, a good morning, a wave, stopping for a chat. These you need to reciprocate to your neighbours.
> – You may need to break the ice yourself.

I have digressed again but thought of telling you this last bit before carrying on with how the setting up of financial plans went.

After arranging our financial matters, the next step was to find out how to upskill and where to get the skill set needed to upgrade. My mum used to say we humans don't stop learning and thus should continually improve our knowledge of whichever work, profession, trade or sport we do. Our brain is a continuous solving machine, operating twenty-four-seven with or without our will. It needs tasks to solve, or it will drift and wander, instead of moving forward.

Our brain is like a fertile garden that grows anything planted. It is so productive that when you do not produce what you like, undesirable weeds will sprout and occupy the empty patch and grow uncontrollably; so it is always important to assign tasks to the brain. This is how you grow intellectually. By improving your education, you can earn more and change work roles. You increase your chances of promotion and give yourself a competitive advantage over other applicants; though it is not a guarantee, it allows you to pursue your passion. You gain self-confidence, wellbeing, job security and satisfaction. You gain a more secure future, a broader knowledge base, and it will help you network with like-minded people.

If you take a good look at yourself, you will find that you always have the appetite for new knowledge to improve yourself. It could be within your field or in a totally new area. In my case, I had a vision I had mapped out in my progress plans before I got into this new country. I based the picture on information I gathered through research and the interview visit.

You do not always see the speed bumps on the road from a fly-past if the speed bumps are not yellow marked. However, you will notice them when you get on the ground and drive on the actual road. That's the point at which you need to adjust your plans. There's a gap between reality and the vision you have for yourself, so you need to build a bridge to cross it. I had set expectations.

The problem was that my expectations were too far away from reality. It is essential not to have too wide a gap as this might lead to anxiety, sadness, discouragement and hopelessness. But it is also crucial to have a gap big enough to keep you challenged and motivated.

After carefully reviewing the upskilling choices I had identified, I enrolled in a study plan that suited my work-life balance. The options were practical but involved sacrificing any leisure time. It did not bother me as experience and observation had taught me that goals can erode if radical changes get ignored. For some people, it might seem daunting and overwhelming to add coursework to your current job, but my advice is that there is no better time to do it than the first few years after landing in a new country.

You recall when I would come from work and head straight to the library or lectures? It is always fulfilling to have your education; no one can take that away from you, except yourself, by remaining static.

You might not have immediate use of the knowledge you gain, or your workplace might not reward you for the new qualification you have earned. However, do not be discouraged and disheartened—you need to tell yourself that whatever self-improvement you have done is for you, and any rewards are a bonus. Your confidence and self-satisfaction are one compensation you will instantly get from the qualification when you complete it.

A short while after I attained my additional qualification in management, the company I work for decided to streamline its staff, as it was experiencing challenges. The organisation conducted a personnel review based on qualifications and experience, and I, with both requirements, never went through the fear, anxiety or depression that some of my colleagues experienced. Peace of mind was one payback that I got years later, and peace of mind is what you will experience whenever you bridge the gap between your reality and your vision. Let me add this to you, Son, an extra qualification will not fully protect you from downsizing if your company decides to do that. It is your track record that will shield you; things like your attendance record; your attitude towards your work, your workmates and your superiors; how you work in a team; your timekeeping abilities and how you adapt to changes or prove your dependability.

> Aspects of your work that will protect you from downsizing:
> – Your attendance record.
> – Your attitude towards your work.
> – Your attitude towards your workmates, superiors included.
> – Your performance in team tasks.
> – Your timekeeping.
> – Your openness to process changes.
> – Your dependability.

My friend shared with me a story about openness to change. He said he had been 'lucky' to have his job still. He got saved by SAP, a type of software used in organisations. I urged him to explain what and how SAP could have saved him. He narrated how his interest in learning led him to familiarise himself with the software before anybody else in his department did. During his break, he would go to another department, where a workmate with whom he had become friends used the software in his daily tasks. He would ask him for all sorts of navigating and transaction codes to use. His superiors noticed his interest in learning other job tasks and created a role for him to perform SAP tasks for his department on top of his regular duties. He was happy to take on the part. So, when the downsizing process came, he was already in a role that would not be affected by changes.

He said that had it not been for his interest in learning new skills through his own initiative, his job would have been on the line. So, he had insulated himself from downsizing shocks well before anyone knew of the impending changes.

Some years back, I led a team of about fifteen staff, including apprentices. The apprentices were fresh from school, starting a new career. The training required them to rotate around all the departments learning all the processes. Among the apprentices was Jody, a South African who had moved from another department; the word was he was a troublemaker, and I needed to keep an eye on him. These were statements made in passing, as no one said anything directly to me.

I found him to be a good student who showed enthusiasm in all the tasks I gave him. Other workers would pass negative comments about him for no apparent reason. I took him under my wing and guided him. I noticed that his timekeeping record had a tiny blemish, which needed clearing up. I had a brotherly talk with him about his timekeeping from the previous department, and he told me his car had issues and so he was using public transport, which was not quite reliable and efficient. No one seemed to understand that. So, I asked him where he lived and noticed I could make a detour on my way to work, adding less than five minutes to my travel time. I told him I would pick him up every morning until he fixed his car. This arrangement worked well, and he was on time until the car repair completion. There was not a single day he was late for the next six months. Somehow, someone decided to terminate his contract because of his previous record.

My point here, Son, is in the employment world, fulfilling your end of the contract is important all the time. Your record is the point of reference for any decision-makers, and you will have no leg to stand on should the organisation decide to lay you off. If you have that blemish and there is no one to represent you other than your record, know that you are gone. Is it cruel? Yes, it wasn't kind. Jody's dream got cut short because someone thought his timekeeping was not good enough, even though he had shown tremendous improvements. In life, there will always be people like the one who cut Jody's dream short without giving him a second chance. However, what is important is the steps and remedial actions that you take after such adversity, which reveal your true character. Challenges peel off the outer casing that covers you and expose the real you.

You can only be a failure if you fail to stand up, dust the dirt off your backside or face and continue your journey. Because life is a trip, a journey, comprising happy and sad moments. No one knows without hesitance the reason we are in the universe. However, whatever the reason, we should enjoy life in its total abundance. The world has all the riches any man can have. If you believe, as I do, that we have been created in the image of the Creator, this should remove any doubt you can have, for a Creator cannot create an image of themselves and want that image to live in poverty, doubt, fear, anxiety, stress, depression and all that makes life unbearable to live—the same as no father or mother would want their offspring to face hardship. The Creator protects as parents protect their children. What separates us as humans from the other species on this planet is our ability to choose our course to happiness.

All our riches are expertly packed, packaged, protected, placed between our ears, and safely guarded by four of the five senses. Eyes to see the enemy, ears and a nose to warn of impending danger, and taste to prevent consuming lousy food that might poison the body and brain. All of these senses direct us to the riches we deserve on this planet.

Zeff was one other apprentice who got let go after completing his training; unlike Jody, he was punctual and completed his tasks well within the specified times. Still, he had one link that he fell 'short' on—his attitude. A positive attitude can land you the role you desperately yearn to have. Attitude can be self-destructive; it is a trait that can be distinctly displayed or wholly folded and stored in the abyss of your inner self that no one can see, except when you bring it out as it suits you. Emotions bring humans to the same level as other species in this universe, like Donovan, our caring, loving canine family member. Donavan has observable feelings of happiness, sadness, anger, and fear like us, depending on what he is experiencing.

However, we humans can choose, direct and control our emotions on our own, meaning we can act with intention, for good or bad. Your surroundings, friends, co-workers, society, environment and family can push those emotional buttons for you too, pushing you to behave in ways that suit or entertain their needs. It is essential to recognise how and who is pushing your buttons and causing you to react the way you do. What came out as a negative attitude from Zeff were responses to pushes on his emotional buttons by co-workers who had identified topics and words that would elicit that behaviour from him. His reaction would be magnified and broadcasted to other departments, and eventually, he got labelled as 'Attitude Zeff'.

After completing his training, heads of departments were asked if anyone would be willing to accommodate him in their departments, and a resounding nay came from everyone. His attitude got noted as the number one factor that had failed him to land a position. His attitude was not consistent with the organisation's set standards. However, measures and standards get abused where judgements are subjective and there's no impartial person there to monitor them, which was the case for both Jody and Zeff.

What would have insulated Zeff from that outcome was his mind. Such scenarios are common, and it's helpful to step back, observe and evaluate the situation and your options, pick the best one and learn from the experience. Zeff's scenario bordered on bullying, which is quite common in workplaces. Knowing your emotional weaknesses, controlling them and disconnecting the loop that attracts tormentors into your life puts you ahead of the pack.

As recently as the beginning of the year 2021, an Independent Police Conduct Authority audit revealed how rampant bullying was in the New Zealand police force, which makes one wonder if there is still a lot of bullying in the police force today. And what about unpoliced workplaces? How are private organisations coping? For example, the police audit noted a 'boys' club' that dominates everything. Anyone not in the club does not get the relaxing treatment and privileges reserved for the club. Similarly, in organisations I worked for, I noted and observed that cases of bullying start with the leader at the top, and the culture cascades down to the shop floor.

I remember coming out from one meeting back then, feeling drawn from how the F-bombs were thrown around in the proceedings. Every second word was a swear word.

I grew up Catholic and was taught not to swear or curse at anything or anyone. Cursing, I was trained, demonstrates a lack of mental capacity and internal turmoil. Each F-word reveals your limited vocabulary and intellect. The words you say have a reverse impact on you. The lousy word you speak to someone is how, subconsciously, you label yourself. I got constantly reminded to use the proper terms rather than the F-word, back in my early years in primary school as well. And I have always kept it in me, deeply embedded in my subconscious mind.

One of the things that lures candidates to join any organisation is the quality of its core values, culture, required behaviours and what the organisation represents. I remember mentioning to an interview panel that I did not take cursing well. Soon after moving my family halfway around the world, I was sitting in meetings where cursing was on display, where it was fashionable to use as many F-words as possible in making your point. 'If it is like this in these meetings, what about the shop floors?' I thought to myself. However, you are only affected by how you relate to a statement and not by the statement itself.

Chapter 4

Honeymoon Period

Multiculturalism, 'ethnic pluralism', or 'a potpourri of ethnicities' is how I would describe the diversity I witnessed in some companies I worked for over the years while gaining exposure and experience. Also, I had the opportunity to observe how respect and values cascade to shop floor levels. To understand life in a cave, one must live in caves. All experiences are valuable, regardless of how they come. My experiences could be anyone's. Pick the lessons that can help you reach a decision. Keep listening; you might stumble upon a nugget along the way worth trading.

Honeymoon periods are usually memorable moments for most couples. A lot of effort ensures the relationship starts on a perfect footing, and good memories are treasured. It is the unflawed, agreeable human side on display. Suppose there was no change after the honeymoon period. That would be remarkable, either for a new workplace or a new couple. One thing you must know is that there is nothing hidden that shall remain hidden, and you will have to deal with whatever is exposed when it is exposed. However, every difference has a solution. It is a tale I will tell you tomorrow, I said to Junior.

You sure need to tell that story, Dad. You look like you are excited about that story with how you are laughing, Junior responded.

I will tell the honeymoon couple story later, for now I will dwell on the workplace, I replied, my brain flooding with past work stories begging to be let out.

The best boss you will ever work for is the one you work for on your first day at work. After that, it will be an unveiling and revelation of the real boss, who may still be a good boss or may be the opposite.

To put into context the team I worked with when I first came over, Dewi was the manager and had migrated from Wales twenty-five years earlier—relatively reserved and came across as detached from his team at times, snobbish, and overly introverted in my early characterisation of him. When I first went for the interview, I remember conversing with him and asking if he was racist. He did not see that coming, and neither did I. Who in their proper sense asks a question like that to their prospective employer unless they do not care about the interview's outcome? Well, it had come from somewhere. It had come from some observation that I had recorded subconsciously that made me ask that question. As much as I wanted to come over into the country, I did not want to go and work with people who viewed other races as inferior. So, I asked him straight up whether he was racist. That question makes a lot of people uncomfortable regardless of their views. I had not planned any questions to ask. His answer was precise as I could see his brain working out the response, and it came out as: 'I do not judge people by the colour of their skin but by their actions and behaviour.' I had heard that phrase somewhere; yes, it was a recital of Martin Luther King's speech. I did not make any follow-up questions along race lines, as I had not intended to ask such questions. However, one was enough to let them know I was sensitive to equality matters.

I had been invited to come over for a one-week interview. Apart from the jet lag, it was fun. I am an introvert and can be in my world and get lost in my thoughts. Like my star sign, the crab, I crawl into my shell. My mum used to call me the 'quiet one' out of my seven siblings. Coster, your uncle, is the opposite of me. He is a motormouth, worse after a beer in his younger days. However, he told me recently that he has learned the habit of listening, which helps him learn from others more than his continuous waffle.

Despite the race questions, Dewi's personality was not entirely different from mine—he was also introverted. The Saturday before I flew back after the interview, Dewi took me on a driving tour down to Rotorua, some two hundred and thirty-one kilometres away, showing me the country's beauty. He took me to his house, and we had dinner with his wife. How a man treats his visitors demonstrates his greatness, generosity and his unveiled, genuine self.

Next to Dewi was Marcus, who had emigrated the year before from Scotland; I would compare him to Coster, except that I couldn't understand half the stuff he was saying because of his heavy Scottish accent most of the time. He couldn't completely understand me either.

He was very affable during my week-long interview; he showed me the neighbourhood, the pubs and the city. On the last day before I flew back to South Africa, I had dinner with him and his wife at O'Hagan, a local gastropub. When he told his wife that I had been offered the position, I vividly remember her saying, 'If Marcus starts giving you grief, just let me know, and I will sort him out.' I burst out laughing, and it was a fun night; I still cherish the memories. What she said was not for me to ask about at the time, but I enjoyed the moment.

One of the conversations I remember having with Marcus was when I told him that I don't take swearing well. That must have made him uncomfortable, as he didn't respond, but he got my message. You cannot change people, but you can tell them who you are and let them decide.

Next down the chain was Popo, an Englishman who, like Dewi, had been in the country for twenty-five years. He was a gentle

Christian who took missionary trips to the islands and did charity work.

Axl was another Englishman but with a strong Cockney accent. His had thirty-five years of service to the organisation. He was a strong Arsenal football team supporter who always walked from the changing room to the car park with an unbuttoned shirt exposing his grey hairy tummy. An interesting character is what I concluded about him. I wondered what Axl would be like to work with in a team.

Next was Taffy, who had come from Wales more than thirty-five years prior. Taffy had also worked for the company for as many years as Axl. In his younger years, he was an acrobat. Taffy was friendly, addressed me as a son and was ready with life advice. He smoked even though he had emphysema; God bless his soul. It's been a decade since Taffy departed this plane, we mortal souls live in momentarily. We are having this conversation in the house he spent his last days. I didn't know this used to be his house until a year after I moved in. On the day I came to view the house, I felt connected to it for some unknown reason, and the real estate agent said the house was mine to move into, in the presence of five other couples in the lounge viewing at the same time as me. Reflecting now, I realise there is more in our life's path than we will ever know. The dots that connect and direct us to our foot trail are invisible but ever-present.

Then there was Nev, of Irish heritage, twenty-five years at the company; Tommy, Sāmoan, twenty-five years also; Cool Kol, who had emigrated from Tonga and worked in the department twenty-three years; Jerry, with a full West-Auckland accent who'd been there twenty-two years; Lip, Dewi's son who'd worked there eight years; and Aiden, Lip's brother who'd been there for two—I soon found out that they called him Snoopy as he was said to be in the habit of reporting co-workers to his dad. He was his dad's third eye. Aiden was still young, fresh out of high school, and excited to be working with Dad as the department's boss.

Then there was Pete, who had been in the department for over thirty years. He was a Māori but could not speak the language as it had been banned when he was growing up. His work assignments were any tasks that required manual handling, even though he was a qualified tradesman. I was told he'd had issues with alcoholism at some point in the past, but no one remembered how far back or the specifics, as the story was passed to every new person who joined the department. That reputation was hanging on his neck like a heavy chain and a log. He stuttered and said little in conversations that veiled more than anyone would ever know about him. I felt something was not quite stacking up; and why the alcoholic story? I needed his story to take home, as he was the only indigenous person in the department. I'm not sure, but maybe he was the reason I had asked Dewi the race question.

The team's composition was very diverse regarding countries of origin. But not so 'diverse' culturally. I was excited to be part of the team. I felt it was a challenge even though everyone had been quite friendly. However, I told myself there was no reason to be afraid of anything other than fear itself.

Integrating into a workplace, school, university or even relationship involves subtle or significant challenges that require overcoming. The differences could be one, two or many. Cultures, personalities, characteristics and behaviours all condense into one homogenous product that should produce and display the desired result. Bringing your own requires gelling with the establishment.

As a new team member, I came into the group with my work ethic, beliefs, culture and perceptions. I arrived with an open mind, or call it a 'beginner's mind', ready to learn, absorb and soak in anything new of 'value'. The issue for us humans is as much as we want to change and assimilate into a new self that will fit into the new setting, the subconscious mind pulls us back from taking the necessary steps for the change to happen. Why? Because it would have taken a lifetime to build and store those beliefs and behaviours. Simple as it may sound to just gell in, we will be bobbing up and down until we can float and swim like everyone in the initial stages.

How the new team member gets incorporated into the new system, workplace or group influences the change in them. The more resistance they have to unlearning other ways of doing things, the more profound the challenge. I worked for the firm's subsidiary in South Africa. So, I assumed I would walk into a standardised orientation practice like I had experienced when I worked for the affiliate company—I also wanted to believe that I would be working with a great team.

And a great team they were. But I soon learned of the differences that can arise from deadlines, work pressures, different leadership concepts and more.

Apart from being introverted, I am also as emotionally sensitive as an elephant. I analyse and evaluate every statement and give it meaning. This can work against me when it becomes overthinking and uses up my mental energy, but it's generally useful. As humans, dealing with other humans, we need to be aware of, and live within boundaries of, acceptable behaviours; beyond that, we slide towards lower levels of life, behaving like animals with thick skins.

It's easy to get entangled in your own web of thoughts when exposed to something that bears no semblance to your own values, more so when the unifier is also the segregator. Like one morning, Popo, the Englishman, was showing me how to complete one of my tasks; Marcus walked by and disparaged Popo's English ethnicity and heritage. It could have been usual banter, but when you notice the receiver not responding, that banter is not banter anymore but sarcasm intended to provoke.

Expressed or unexpressed emotions manifest in our behaviour even when we try to hide them.

Getting fun out of annoying others is just as bad as physical harm, for annoyance affects the heart, generating pesky emotions.

What divides humanity is not origin, borders, language or colour but ignorance, perception and fed misinformation; what a better world it would be if every person would take a moment to reflect before saying or doing anything that offends another? Just take a moment to ask whether you would be happy if the other person told you what you are about to say. Would I be pleased if the other person were in my position and treated me the way I am about to treat them? Would I be happy if the other person were in my place and denied me the chance to progress in life? Would I be pleased if the other person denied me the opportunity to learn a new skill? Would I be happy if the other person spread false information about me? Would I be pleased if the other person were in my position and denied me time off when I needed the time off? Swapping positions, putting yourself in the shoes of the less fortunate, then working to correct how you see the world from their perspective would make this world better than it is now.

The universe has the habit of returning to you what you have done to others in kind. The universe may not return to you what you have given in its exact form, but be sure to know that it knows how to classify your deed and compensate your worth.

If you make another person angry, someone will make you angry. If you make another person happy, someone will make you happy. If you donate money, be assured that the universe will return it to you threefold. If you cheat on your partner, wife or husband, know that the favour will get returned at some point. If you steal, someone will steal from you. Above all, make peace with everyone. Always apologise if you unintentionally hurt someone. You do not want any person to have an emotional scar caused by your actions or inaction.

Practise adding value to the next person and making their life better, whether they are a friend, fellow worker, subordinate, boss, girlfriend, wife or brother. Compliment them. Son, always say something positive to leave the conversation with a smile. A smile on their face is also a smile on your face.

Say something to leave them with a smile:
- You are a fantastic friend, a fantastic person; I feel lucky to know a person like you.
- I like your style.
- I enjoy having a conversation with you.
- You are a great person.
- You are my family.
- You make me happy.
- You have all my respect.
- I will always respect your opinion.
- You are my favourite person to spend time with.
- You are incredible.
- You inspire me to be a better person.
- Your passion always motivates me.
- Your smile makes me smile.
- The way you carry yourself is genuinely admirable.
- You are such a good listener.
- You have a remarkable sense of humour.
- Thanks for being you.

- You set an excellent example for everyone around you.
- I love your perspective on life.
- Being around you makes everything better.
- You are one of a kind.
- You make me want to be the best version of myself.
- You always have the best ideas.
- I am so lucky to have you in my life.
- Your capacity for giving has no boundaries.
- I wish I were more like you.
- Your kindness is natural and overflowing like a waterfall.
- You have such a great heart.
- Knowing you has made me a better person.
- You are unique to everyone here.
- You are beautiful inside and out.
- Your heart must be twice the average size.
- You are my favourite person to talk to.
- I always learn so much when I am around you.
- You are the person that everyone wants on their team.

Practise conversation generosity such that others feel they can talk to you whenever the need beckons.

'Who cares?', 'I don't care' and 'Nobody cares' are the other choices we have as humankind. Erase these phrases out of your vocabulary. The universe cares for what you do not care about and will care to return that 'I don't care' in the exact form and expression you have said it.

Whenever you feel negative emotions because of a difference in thinking, ask yourself if it is 'necessary' to respond in this way. Is it necessary that I must blow off my top for this? Is it necessary that I suspend my happiness? Is it necessary to be angry? Is it necessary that I must be resentful? When faced with a situation that begs you to think small, always wear the big wisdom cap, skip trivial matters, and grow big by thinking big and thinking as your hero would think.

My supervisor, Marcus, came up with a brilliant team-building idea. A couple of weeks before Christmas is when I joined the team full-time—the best time to join a team and the worst. We went bowling and laser-tagging; it was a brilliant night. Everyone who turned up loved it so much that it became a monthly thing for a couple of months, then died on the third. Authentic characters and personalities usually come out when people are at a social gathering. Words and statements that wouldn't come out in controlled settings are let out.

I was rubbish on the first outing, and everyone enjoyed my misses and ducks. I then got better the next and the next. Then I remember excitedly saying at work after the outing how good I had become. To which Marcus said, 'You must have been practising.'

I replied, laughing, 'No! Not at all.'

Then he retorted, 'I don't trust aliens anyway,' with a scowling face.

It was shocking to hear that from my supervisor, to my face. I had ignored some statements in passing, but this one had found a reason to stay. Subtle comments run back to a person's core. I had been in the country for less than three months and had just been called an 'alien'. Yes, I was, and so was he. We were all non-natives in that sense. He had been in the country just a year longer than me, which would have made him an alien in that sense too. I was the odd one out. I looked different from everyone, so that qualified me as an alien and him not. Or did it?

The conversation had been general between a supervisor and his subordinate, or so I thought. The scene was next to our department tearoom; no one was there, only the two of us. What was I to do? Confront him? No. He had walked away soon after the statement to end the conversation. The oversensitivity in me was overtaking my self-control. The relations were going down a slippery slope. I needed his support as well as his guidance to perform my duties effectively. But I did not need to be labelled an alien among fellow human beings. How we choose to give meaning to a statement affects us. If you give it a meaning, it affects you. Ignore it, and no effect happens to you.

I thought, *I am new in this country, and I have a contract tying me to this department for five years. If I raise it with our boss or HR, I cannot transfer to another department, and it would be my word against Marcus's.* Leaving the company would mean repaying the relocation expenses, which were quite a considerable sum. I got promoted to the role of team leader within the first three months. My team had long-serving staff members, and most had worked in the department for more than twenty-five years. They all were from the Northern Hemisphere, and were my dad's generation and older. My co-workers came with some deep-seated beliefs and biases that were waiting for validation through self-prophecy in my actions, I began analysing my situation. That was the difficulty that lay at the root of my problem. I had younger team members, but they were seniors in the company, and two of my subordinates were the boss's sons. So, the decision to promote me did not get accepted across the plant—I was an alien now, by myself.

When odds get stacked against your favour, let go of the challenge for a later date. Learn to swim in shallow waters before going to the deep end. My mental health was under severe testing most days; I relinquished the role I had been given but remained in the department and was assigned to work under one of the long-serving staff, Axl, as my team leader. Axl was known for his bulldog character, tearing, dressing down and humiliating subordinates.

I later learned Axl had been cautioned to tone it down when addressing co-workers several times in the past.

One day he came to me from the office, excitedly saying, 'This time, Africans are coming on their own, unlike before, when they got captured and forced onto boats.' Meaning *I* had come on my own, a statement that reflected his inner thoughts. I walked away, not wanting to dwell on it and give him the satisfaction he wanted from my reaction.

On another occasion, he tore me apart in front of everyone a few days later for reasons known only to himself. I could not take that anymore, and I went straight to Human Resources (HR) and told the HR manager that I wanted to return to my country. I couldn't stand this humiliation and degradation. The HR manager told me it would be sad if I left my workmates. 'They like you,' he had said. Then he asked if anyone had called me the N-word, to which I told him none had done so. He knew about Axl's reputation, and I am sure he knew what was happening. HR had a meeting with Axl, and not long after the meeting, Axl went on retirement. He was seventy-two and had been thinking about retirement for a while.

A good friend of mine who was writing a book on diversity in workplaces asked me years later what it was like in my early years in this country. I blurted out, 'Deep South.' Of course, I don't know much about the Deep South of the United States of America apart from the movies I had watched. But I felt I experienced a milder, veiled version of that.

Was I getting lost in my evaluation of the circumstances I found myself in or was it real? I had experienced the 'good man' in most of these guys. Unfortunately, the display of one's 'negative' character overshadows their good. The bad side tends to stay and have a party when the good side has left. What is it that becomes important to us? Is it the eighty percent good displayed most of the time or the twenty percent deficient? Or should there be such an imbalance in us? Many people in abusive relationships ignore the wrong part and try to live with the good part until the 'bad' part becomes intolerable. They would then leave with deep emotional or, worse, physical scars.

When I relinquished the role, my replacement came from my part of the world, but looked a bit more like everyone else. That made me pay attention and observe the goings-on in the department from a vantage point. I knew I had been thrown in the deep end. My supervisor agreed that was what he had done. Why had he thrown me to wolves? Had I been a project?

Pierre, who replaced me, was brought in the same way; relocation expenses were paid and bonded to the department and organisation for five years. However, it became evident that it was not the melanin difference, as I and others had thought, that caused difficulties. Instead of unifying the department, subtle comments were constantly used to maintain ethnic, historical and heredity divisions.

In most work environments, it is not the tasks, duties and deadlines that make people hate their workplace, if they ever do. It is the co-workers. It is the co-workers that make us enjoy work. It is the team that you work with day in and day out. The friendships that grow and develop through common goals. The goal is to achieve a collective outcome. As Marcus Aurelius Antoninus said, 'For we are made for cooperation, like feet, like hands, like eyelids, like the rows of the upper and lower teeth. To act against one another is then contrary to nature.' So are we in whatever team we are placed.

Everyone who performs tasks to achieve an organisation's set goals is a team member regardless of job title or rank. The woman or man at the top must create an inclusive, friendly environment. That person should be able to say unconsciously, 'I am worthy of my habits imitated by my subordinates.' I have worked for several organisations and observed, experienced and noted that those who do well are the ones who value workers' cultures and differences.

One of the tasks I set myself to do over the last few years was to expose myself to other organisations' cultures. Get a side job in an afternoon shift role and work on a shop floor. Once again, experience the treatment new immigrants get in a different setting and compare it to my initial experiences. Few people look like me in this country, less than 0.3 percent. It is easy to quickly gauge how people like me are treated and compare it to my first experiences. On one such assignment, I was forced to raise my concerns over the unfairness after an unpleasant experience.

It was a fries-making factory, the opposite of all the work settings I had been exposed to in my work life. So, it became my first experience as a gender minority in an organisation. The lady supervisor I was assigned to work under was quite a unit and of Tongan descent. She must have been a rugby prop in her younger days. *Tough looking and devoid of friendliness*, I thought the first time we locked eyes.

You should know that no matter how tough someone presents themselves, there is always a suppressed soft, cuddly baby inside them. Most bullies are like that. Tough-looking outside and jelly inside. All you need to do is confront and stand your ground. That's how you take away bullies' fun. The more you get visibly offended by their taunting, the more they devise ways to provoke you. Size does not matter in the workplace. Rules and regulations matter, and bullies know that.

At this job, I was supposed to change task station every hour. Job tasks were designed to limit the repetitive strain of the chore and refresh the worker to perform at their maximum capacity.

I was aware of this process but did not get moved for unknown reasons. Hertha, the Supervisor, continually assigned me to all the menial tasks despite there being five other workers in the same role. She never explained much about the duties she gave, which reminded me of Pete at my other job, who had been given all the jobs requiring manual handling.

When floating in the negative zone, it is easy to attract similar people to yourself. A negative person and a negative person double the negative energy. Nothing positive comes from two or more negative people unless one changes their frequency to affect the other. At some point in our lives, we fall into 'negative' zones despite our efforts to be in the positive.

We are experts, subconsciously, when it comes to judging others on first meetings. Before any conversation, we measure our energy and frequency levels, then adjust fields to match each other. To subdue or dominate the other. After a verbal exchange, we feel the aura levels in that new environment.

Hertha gave me a task in a contemptuous way, a tone of voice and a sneer I felt was quite disrespectful to anyone. I went on to tell her, 'That's not the way to speak to another human being; every person deserves to be respected the same way as you do, Hertha.' And added, 'I have been in this country for the past fourteen years, I have a full-time job elsewhere; I am here for the experience, and thanks for the experience.' Before I finished the statement, the Shift Manager walked in.

When I explained what had transpired to the Shift Manager, Ho, who was of Chinese heritage, he interjected and told us to calm down. He gave me a task elsewhere for the rest of the shift. The following day I did not turn up for my shift roster. My employment agent rang to tell me Ho wanted me to come back. I would be reporting to him, not the Supervisor. When I returned the following day, I got assigned a new role of monitoring and recording process fluctuations, a comfortable position. The treatment had swung one hundred and eighty degrees. I enjoyed the work so much that I looked forward to my shift. Hertha became friendly and smiley after the incident. She shifted me from the box she thought I belonged in, the rookie unsure of everything. I worked for another six months and then quit. The treatment had changed for the good. Instead of becoming a victim, I had dictated my terms. There was nothing new to experience and learn, so I abandoned the mission. Ho would call me for one-off shifts if I wanted to work.

That experience revealed that some people in charge take advantage of subordinates who lack knowledge of their rights or are insecure, because of prejudice. Hertha, the Supervisor, assumed I was desperate and would take any insults she threw at me. She was probably basing that on her experiences with other staff that had worked under her. Hertha could have been in the process of returning the treatment she herself had encountered somewhere along her path. It could be one of many reasons. Not every subordinate will challenge their boss's leadership style unless that subordinate is secure and knowledgeable of their rights.

Some years back, while upskilling, I met Mike, who had been out of employment for more than two years. His story was that he had immigrated on a work visa like me and had, after an issue with his employer, quit the job, and could not land another as his former employer had blacklisted him. Every time he went for a job interview, he got declined after the former boss's negative reference popped up.

The law did not protect many employees like Mike or myself back in those days. You had to roll with the punches until you received your permanent residence visa. Some wicked bosses took advantage of the power they had over migrant workers. Though the situation has changed a lot, you still hear of isolated exploitation cases now and then.

In those days, an employee brought in under the employer-assisted visa got bonded to the employer until the contract expired or they obtained a residence visa, exposing the migrant worker to the employer's mercy. Hence Axl's comments.

You had to be smart like Mike, who, instead of wallowing in misery and feeling sorry for himself, went on to study and got an MBA, then crossed over the ditch and started a new and better life using the education he had acquired while the former boss thought he had the key to Mike's future, taking away his livelihood. Out of resistance and struggle comes strength. Through adversity, you grow if you have the will and desire to escape the situation. His thinking guided his intelligence, and his brightness was much more potent than the bad references of someone keen on taking away his God-given right to peace, joy and happiness. His spirit remained unconquered, and he rose above the drawbacks and limitations.

It is stories like Mike's that I am passing on to you, Son. Whatever the situation you find yourself in, there is always an alternative to remediate your situation. The possibilities are within you. You hold the key to the exit door in any circumstance.

You will never be a victim of circumstances unless you believe you are. When you fall, you stand up, like you did when you got your first skateboard from Amy, my workmate, when you were four. The same determination and passion you had to learn to skate should always drive you throughout your life. We fall, stand up, fall and stand up until we can glide and do tricks. We live to think and think to live and live to change and change to live; such is the circle until we depart. Strive to be a better person than you were yesterday, and the incremental changes you implement will make you a happier person down the path of life.

It always requires effort to produce a good yield when harvest time comes. It is the early rises and the late finishes. Twelve or more hours of toiling in cold or hot weather do not make a difference for the farmer. What makes the difference is the yield. So, it should be in you; always picture the outcome and be driven by the passion and desire to have it in your possession. Remember, a seed of maize does not produce one grain of maize or its equivalent number, but it multiplies several hundred times. Do not be discouraged by the effort you put into getting to your yield. For you shall get rewarded in great abundance. The universe always rewards someone who sets out to improve themself. Through your improvement, the universe improves.

Our past experiences always prepare us to approach, deal and resolve similar scenarios in the future should they arise. However, the ability to recognise and relate to past similar events and make informed decisions separates the mediocre from those who excel in whatever they do. Scenarios do not always repeat themselves in the exact form or shape.

In any situation that requires your input, know that there is always some takeaway. It is for your purpose or for someone else who needs your guidance. I am passing on my experiences to you, Son, so that you are better equipped than I was.

> The universe always rewards someone who sets out to improve themself. Through your improvement, the universe improves.

After I left the fries-making factory, I asked my employment agent to find me another assignment, which he did in no time. He gave a brief description of the organisation before giving me the assignment. He knew about my main job and the basis of my second job. He said the assignment had interesting workers and would benefit my mission. I said, 'Bring it on, brother.'

The afternoon roster was from 4:30 pm to 10:30 pm. It was an insulation-making company. The tasks involved lifting finished insulation products from the conveyor belt to a storage location, which required four people at the end of the conveyor. When the insulation sheet comes off from the production machine, you jointly roll it, the four of you, and put the rolls into plastic bags. Every four minutes, a sheet will come through; a lapse by any one of the individuals would affect the whole team. Uniformity was necessary to accomplish the task. Machine speed was adjustable depending on production and customer needs.

Safety was next to zero. No earmuffs nor face masks were provided to muffle noise and prevent dust particle inhalation. You could also smell urine stink in the tearoom not far from the toilet. Overalls or work clothes were not mandatory; any clothes would do. A gang member clad in his fully embellished leather jacket and sleeveless T-shirt was part of my first shift assignment. Most shift crew members had tattoos on their faces and bodies. However, what I discovered about this crew was that they were all very friendly. It was 'Howzit, bro', 'Hey bro', 'What's up, bro.' They all made me feel welcome despite their intimidating appearances.

There were indeed 'interesting' characters, and I bet some stories behind those characters too, which I wanted to hear. But, unfortunately, the smoko was a standard fifteen minutes; one person at a time, all rotating, so there was no time for sitting down and having a group chat or talk.

I am sure they wanted to hear my story, too. Rangi, the one in the gang jacket, asked for my phone number, which I somehow managed not to give him. I wasn't sure why I refused to give him my number, but it must be some prejudice and perception I had against gang members. Had he not been wearing the gang patches, I probably would have given him my number. I probably looked like someone who could somehow fit in their unit, but I didn't know how or what role I would play.

The following day I rang up my agent, Jackie, to let him know that I was uncomfortable returning to that assignment because of the unsafe working conditions. He told me to hang on until he sourced another opening for me. He said he would call me as a stand-by person for that assignment, to which I agreed. The next time he asked me to go to that same assignment was two weeks later, on an early Saturday morning.

I had just finished my ten-kilometre Saturday run and was about to get into my car. The phone rang, and Jackie pleaded for me to go to the insulation place. I said, 'Nah, I won't be able to go; I have just finished my run. I would not be ready until after about an hour.'

Still, he persisted that I should go. 'They desperately need a fourth person. They will wait for you; please, brother, help us on this one.' So, I drove home, took a hot shower, and had a full breakfast even though I limited myself in what I ate on Saturdays. I knew the task ahead was not an easy one.

Driving there, I wondered whether I would meet with the crew I had worked with on my first assignment or a new one. Finally, I got to the place at the forty-five-minute mark.

I wore the hi-vis top that I had brought along, as well as ear-muffs, goggles and face masks that Jackie had provided. I had raised my concerns about the safety and noise level, and Jackie had noted it. I am safety conscious and know that no substitute will be as effective and efficient as your body parts. Hence it is of prime importance to protect your body from any harm.

As I walked in, I expected the heavily tattooed, gang-patched guys like on the last assignment, but it was quite the opposite: these workers were meek-looking but friendly.

A pattern emerged in all the workplaces I worked in, including my primary company. However, I still wasn't quite sure whether this pattern was in my head, or if it was real. The pattern was that a worker was seen as a tool that complements a machine to produce an output. The worker's service was all that mattered, not the totality or comprehensive package that comes with the service, the human being, and the person. Workers think they work to have a better life. But life will never be better as all the things that make life are what every individual already has. Being alive, consciousness, is life. A combination of the exposure and experience that humans seek is what allows them to learn, teach, grow and evolve as humans. It is not a better life, but it is what opens awareness, consciousness and purpose for living. Misidentified as a better life. The better life misconception leads to greed, overindulgence, deceit, injustice, envy, treachery, recklessness or malice. Which are the opposite of what a better life is.

I had a good shift but was quite exhausted at the end of the day. I needed my weekend and would prefer something not as taxing as this assignment in the future. There was little interaction, and tea breaks had the same setup as the afternoon shift.

The supervisors treated me like their own, the two times I had been to this place. The tasks needed the full cooperation of everyone, and there was no rest time in between. Everyone I had worked with on these two shifts had their mission and was concerned primarily about completing the shift and getting paid at the end of the week, and there were no dramas in between. I would have wanted to come for more 'shifts' at this premises, but, *Nah*, I said to myself, *Ask for a different location*.

The following Monday, I rang Jackie and said, 'Find me another place. The work is heavy and tiring at the insulation place.'

To which he concurred. 'Most of the guys I send to that place never want to return, so I agree.'

A couple of weeks later, he rang me excitedly and asked, 'Do you want to work this coming weekend?'

'Yeah... Nah. Where?' I asked flatly.

'Easy job, brother, good people, good hours,' he said. 'Let's meet at this address on Saturday at 11 am; I will show you the place, we'll discuss the time, and then decide.'

I got to the place a few minutes before 11 am. Three other guys had come for the same job. It was a logistics company that received and distributed prepared meals. The reception area, the tearoom, and the toilets were top-notch—quite the opposite of the last assignment. My tasks involved packing boxes according to destination area codes. The packages were shipped right across the upper part of the country by trucks. It was a repetitive job, with lots of idle time in between, and lots of interaction. Good for a core workout, I thought as I looked at the physical benefit of the task. My day job involved sitting most of the time; hence I enjoyed my Saturday morning runs. Most boxes weighed less than ten kilograms; any fit person could do the task.

The permanent staff were ladies and a fellow who gave us a quick tour of performing the tasks. All excellent, friendly crew. At the end of my six-hour shift, Glenda, one of the permanent staff, thanked us and asked if we could come back the following day, to which I declined as I wanted to have Sunday to myself. I was going to come back again the next Saturday anyway. There was no misalignment in our field zones, and I clicked with the team. They were free with answers to any questions I asked. Ray, the Manager, told me, 'Sunday deliveries are by private cars; you can come tomorrow if you want.'

'I will do Saturday and Sunday the following weekend: I have something tomorrow,' I said.

'That's fine; we will see you on Saturday,' Ray replied.

I had made a mark by showing interest in their business. I probably had the attributes of the person they wanted, I thought. Simultaneously, I reminded myself that I wasn't there for the long haul; I wasn't there for a career change, but to gain exposure. The following weekend, the shift would start at 10 am, so I received a text about the changes during the week. It was all good with me as I had set aside plans for that weekend.

I was there, smack-bang on time, at 10 am when Saturday came. I knew the tasks I would perform, so I commanded myself like an experienced logistics person. Inwards goods receipting with scanners and storing in the allocated bins. The manager came over to share a cuppa and chat on my break. All week I had been thinking of the private car delivery opportunity. So I asked Ray, 'How do I go about it if I wanted to do deliveries?'

He said it was easy. 'I would put your name down on the list. You would then do one-day training. After that, you get the uniforms and start deliveries as a courier driver.'

'Easy!' I said. 'Put my name down. When is the training?' I asked gingerly.

'Next Tuesday,' he answered.

'I am set for Tuesday!' I said happily, which was the start of my new career as a weekend courier driver.

My Peugeot 407 black coupe was a bit flashy to be a courier car, but it didn't bother me; all I now wanted was to experience life as a courier driver. The business model was that drivers would use their cars as delivery cars and then get paid for the number of boxes they delivered in a zone—option one of payment. Ray had said he would get me to 'deliver' closer to the depot, which meant I would make more trips. Option two was that the further away from the depot you deliver the boxes, the more money you get per box.

I did my math with the estimated boxes I would deliver per day. But the time I would take to drop off each package needed to be added to the equation.

I used an application that had to be downloaded on my phone and linked to Google Maps for addresses. I used my phone, internet data, car and labour.

'Awe-inspiring business model,' I muttered. The first weekend I delivered closer to the depot. I completed a couple of trip loads, but moving from one location to the next took me forever. Google Maps would take me the long way at times, even though the app arranged the addresses chronologically. I do not swear because of my upbringing. Had that not been the case, it would have been a day of cursing and swearing.

That day I recalled one of my apprentices, Brooke, whom I had worked with in my earlier years in this country. She had noticed my lack of swearing in the face of frustration and would urge me to swear. She would say, 'Go on, Maxwell, it is okay, let it out; you are allowed to swear when you are frustrated,' but no lousy word would escape from my mouth despite the encouragement. There was only a lot of muttering and exasperated 'Oh man! Oh man!' frustration, which was the case on this day. It took me eight hours to complete the deliveries, a full working day. By the end of the day, I was exhausted and frustrated. But the experience had been worthwhile. Throughout the day, I met several great folks. Most were glad I had brought them their food for the weekend and some for the week. Some were keen to hold a more extended conversation than necessary, so I would politely tell them I still had more deliveries to complete. Some were surprised and happy to have their food box delivered in a flashy car. I left most addresses with a big smile, for smiling is contagious.

The following weekend I asked Ray if he could give me option two deliveries, as I wanted to compare the payments and the time it would take to complete them, to which he agreed.

In everything you do, Son, every decision you make should be based on complete information. It is always wise to do research first and fill in missing gaps as they appear. It is essential to ask yourself what you are learning from your actions. What is it that you learned from your last activities?

Insufficient preparation, doubt and lack of self-confidence are common elements that make us overwhelmed by tasks. Please don't fall into that ditch as I did, for I have been in that ditch before. Anything challenging in this world has been experienced and overcome by someone; blessed ones get forewarned of life's pitfalls.

Blessed are those who receive unsolicited life advice. As fathers and mothers, we must pass down all experiences, good or bad, to our children, for that is how we leave this world a better place. I got told that kids need to learn and experience what parents went through at some point. But if all kids had to go through what their parents went through, would we live the lifestyle we have today? No. People would still be living in the open, probably not even in caves. So next time you hear me say, 'Gone are the days', Junior, say to me, 'Enjoy the present'.

After I finished my long route, option-two deliveries, I rang Ray and thanked him for arranging my tasks for that day. I knew I had gained what I wanted to learn should I venture into a similar business. I compared the courier wages for the two weekends' work that I had done the following Thursday after getting paid. I evaluated the amount of time, fuel, mobile data, and wear and tear on my car. I found neither was better than the other. It was six of a one and half a dozen of the other, the same. I would claim tax back on using my vehicle, but it was not worth continuing as a learning and a weekend job. The purpose of all my second jobs was always to learn and experience work outside my regular job. Money was not the objective purpose, although it would have enticed me to continue working for a bit. I left the courier job richer than what I had been paid. I still possess what I earned, and the value of the experience will always stay with me.

My Technology Dean, years back in college, used to lecture us about the importance of working smarter, not harder. He used to say you need to identify your competitive advantage all the time and maximise that advantage to reach your goals quicker, and for self-growth. That philosophy worked well for my temporary courier job and others. How motivated you are is what drives your performance output. So, it was easy for Ray to say, yep, I can put your name forward, and you can start as soon as you want. Ray must have seen my confidence and zeal in all the tasks he had assigned me those two weekends before deliveries.

We have industrious people in this country who live busy lifestyles, and most are grateful for the kind of life they live. I concluded this after the deliveries.

I had one isolated case who complained about the delivery when I got to her place. I smiled at her politely and told her I would convey her complaints to the bosses, and encouraged her to call them should it take longer than anticipated to get any feedback. If someone gives you lemons, make lemonade and enjoy the drink. If you pass on the lemons to someone without using them, you will have missed an excellent opportunity to learn from the experience.

Over the first few years, I became resentful and angry due to unmet expectations. I regretted the choice I had made to emigrate here. But I asked myself where else I would have gone. I know I could have gone to another country other than this one. But how sure was I that I would not experience the same challenges there? New Zealand had been top on my list of favoured countries. One of the drawbacks of migrating to some other countries was language. We were going to start learning a new language, me and your mum—it would not be so hard for yourself, as kids can learn faster. It was going to be a monumental challenge for us, compared to the one at hand. My thoughts calmed down.

I was raised Catholic, but I neglected or abandoned my faith along the way when I migrated, which I found was not uncommon.

That faith would have carried me through the challenges I faced and given me an extra cushion. The critical part was forgiveness for myself and the 'perpetrators'. But the most crucial factor was the power to know that I could change whatever was happening in my life. Growing up and going to school, I got taught that knowledge is power, and I remember my school badge had *knowledge is power* on it. I got told that when you have an education, you possess power. But I missed the part that says for knowledge to be power, it needs organisation. Having degrees and diplomas lining up your living room walls is not power, but how the knowledge gets organised to better yourself and the world is power.

Fretting, fussing, and fuming does not resolve anything; it makes the issues at hand worse. If not worse, then it becomes a vicious cycle, with every day bringing similar problems. Not because of the people you work with, deal with, and surround yourself with, but because of y-o-u-r-s-e-l-f.

Your knowledge is not power but your worst enemy, if you do not know how to organise it and make it work for you, your family and society at large.

As a father, I know I have always said that children need to be better than their parents. Yes, in every way. These are some expectations, and unnecessary pressure, that parents put on their kids. I have been comparing your achievements to mine at your age. I have every reason to believe that you are on your path to your calling, and you will achieve according to your set goals, not my goals. I will guide you when I notice you are falling off the rails. Most of the time, you assure me and say, 'I have got this, Dad.'

When I talk of rails, I know you might think the rails of life I used when I was your age do not apply nowadays. They are probably rusty and warped due to the length of time since they got first laid down. But let me assure you that these rails will always be ageless. They are the guiding principles of life. Regardless of which part of the world you live in, how much money you have in the bank, the house you live in, the mode of transport you use or your status in society, they will always apply, and they define your worth as a human being. The guiding principles sit within your soul. You can find more of them if you search within yourself.

These are being compassionate, accepting, having integrity, and evolving with the universe.

Being compassionate is treating the other as an extension of yourself, wanting the best out of the next person regardless of their background. Acceptance is acknowledging that some things are beyond your control and being grateful for what you have now. Integrity is being the observer and monitor of your behaviours, habits, ways, or practices and holding yourself accountable for the outcomes. Evolving with the universe is continuously improving yourself and not dwelling in the past. Falling off the rails leads to self-inflicted unhappiness and pain.

The Rails of Life:
– Compassion
– Acceptance
– Integrity
– Evolving with the universe

We get bogged down by worrying about what other people think of us instead of focusing on the task. We all love ourselves more than anyone. Why, then, do we care about other people's opinions about us? In future, Son, whenever such worry encroaches your mind, tell yourself that whatever anyone thinks of you is none of your business. Your business is to do what you must do successfully. Remember, we cannot read anyone's thinking unless that thinking is in the process of manifesting into a thing. At that point, you can only make a defensive move to guard yourself against being psychologically harmed. In all my thirty years of work experience, I have not witnessed nor heard of anyone who got physically harmed in a workplace setting. It is always the barking, not the biting, in most workplaces, for the rules and regulations are clear on dealing with the biting ones, not much on the barking ones. The barking ones get protected as they are perceived to shoo off intruders and protect their owners, just like Donovan, my canine son.

We can comfortably leave the house the whole day or night unlocked if Donovan is well-fed and healthy; no intruder will burgle us. Our possessions will be safe. Such is what most organisations are like; unrestrained barking if no one is complaining. Some organisations have 'collars' that control the barking. Like you know how we got that dog collar for Donovan when he was a puppy to control his barking after Barry, the back-neighbour, had complained? The collar would zap him and activate an electric shock each time he barked, which in my mind was inhumane; poor Donovan's fun got taken away. I felt sorry for him, but we had to do it as the dog control unit had rung me about the complaint.

It worked for a while and soothed Barry, the neighbour, too, or so I thought.

And then, one day after work, I got home and took off the collar. It must have been the opportunity Donovan had been looking forward to, to get freed from the zapper. After removing the zapper, I put it beside me on the stoop where I was sitting, and suddenly my phone rang in the house. I went to get the phone and answered the call; when I got back, Donovan had chewed the zapper. An intelligent dog, we all concurred, and that was how Donovan freed himself. It was an expensive device and cruel. I was reluctant to replace it and gave Donovan back his freedom.

The zappers in the workplace are an organisation's values and principles, not inhuman like Donavan's. They protect vulnerable people and must be worn around the necks of those who bark more than necessary. In most workplaces, they are in place, but some businesses do an excellent job of keeping them idle and will only produce them as evidence when a complaint gets raised. Rules and regulations make it mandatory to have the vulnerable protected. Every newbie who enters a workplace should familiarise themselves with company zappers, which should happen during induction. They give good protection to both the newbie and the company. There is a lot of emphasis on safety in workplaces now, compared to ten or twenty years ago. Organisations are held accountable by governments should they breach safety regulations. Employee education on safe work practices is pivotal in adhering to these regulations. Many businesses and companies ensure they do not fall short of mandatory expectations; in most places I have worked, I have seen lockout and tag-out systems to protect workers from getting electrocuted or crushed by machinery under maintenance. I have witnessed barriers that protect pedestrians from using the same path as moving machinery like fork hoists. I have seen fire alarm systems, witnessed spill kits, and seen weekly or monthly safety audits in place. I have conducted these audits myself.

I have also seen Equal Employment Opportunity statements saying this company is an equal-opportunity employer and quoting the Human Rights Act 1993. However, I have not seen in all these workplaces alarm systems, barriers or audits enacted for *emotional* safety. I have not ever had an induction that directly mentions emotional safety. There is always talk and emphasis that workers should go home in the same state as they come to work, and no doubt it applies to physical harm. Workers get repeatedly reminded to wear their protective equipment to minimise exposure to hazards that can cause serious workplace injuries and illnesses. These injuries and conditions may result from chemical, radiological, physical, electrical or mechanical causes, such as noise, dust, fumes or other workplace hazards.

All workers should have tools and equipment that protect them from emotional harm in workplaces, like the standard PPE. They should also constantly get reminded to use their protective gear against emotional harm. In most factories, a toolbox safety talk gets done at the beginning of the day or shift, where workers get reminded of the hazards ahead. Those talks should include the emotional aspect of safety, which will only sound counter-intuitive if the perpetrator is the one who is giving the safety toolbox talk.

Could it be why the emotional health safety aspect gets avoided? The Human Rights Act 1993 does cover it broadly. Still, organisations need to break the act down, so it becomes easy to identify actions and inactions potentially detrimental to emotional safety.

You may be wondering and asking what these human rights I am talking about are. I am not a lawyer like my cousin Kenny. However, I will explain what the legal Act covers, so that you know your rights.

Equal Opportunity in New Zealand, The Human Rights Act 1993 (HRA) and the Employment Relations Act 2000 were enacted to help ensure that all workplaces are safe and fair. This legislation covers the many forms of discrimination regarding sexual harassment and unjust treatment in the workplace. While the policies mainly protect employees, they also protect job applicants, contractors and people associated with them, such as family carers and friends.

According to the Human Rights Act 1993, it is unlawful for anyone to get discriminated against because of age, race or skin colour, gender or sexual orientation, marital status, physical or mental disability, family or care responsibilities, pregnancy, religion or political opinion, national extraction or social origin.

> It is unlawful to discriminate based on:
> – Age
> – Race or skin colour
> – Gender or sexual orientation
> – Marital status
> – Physical or mental disability
> – Family or care responsibilities
> – Pregnancy
> – Religion or political opinion
> – National extraction or social origin

The Human Rights Commission is the organisation that promotes and protects the human rights of all people in this country. It works under the Human Rights Act 1993 to lead, evaluate, monitor and advise on all matters regarding equal employment opportunities.

Suppose you believe you have not been given equal workplace opportunities under this Act. You can complain to the commission for advice and support, and you need not worry about payment as it is all free, flexible and confidential.

If the complaint is unresolved through their usual process, the case goes to the Human Rights Review Tribunal.

Employers have a clear duty of care to prevent discrimination,

> If you believe you have not been given equal opportunities under the Human Rights Act, you can complain to the Human Rights Commission for advice and support. It is free and confidential.

harassment and victimisation in the workplace, failure of which can result in severe penalties.

Businesses must also have a written policy covering the priorities placed on equal opportunity, which must be regularly reviewed and updated to reflect changes to legislation or company culture.

I have come across these statements in some organisations I have worked for over the past years. However, as I have said, no emphasis is given in these statements regarding employee education; probably, it's a necessary evil that needs displaying for regulatory purposes only.

In my early years in this country, I found out that even though the legislation act got displayed on the notice boards, no one spoke of or mentioned anything about that Act, despite the flouting and trampling of worker rights in the department where I was a waged employee.

When I got promoted to a salaried position, I got exposed to my 'rights'. The 'right' that every employee has to be educated.

The education comprised videos and a test to get a yearly diploma covering harassment and workplace bullying. Unfortunately, the organisation prioritised the training for the salaried staff only, which I found perplexing; keeping the lower-level workers ignorant of their rights perpetuated a culture of bullying and the trampling of employee rights. I heard statements that employees in this country are docile compared to our 'cousins' across the ditch, but it was contrary to reality, as some employees are not docile but ignorant of their worker rights.

Most migrant workers come from countries where worker rights are non-existent or ignored, and when they come over here, the money they earn is enough to put them off reporting some of the workplace abuses they experience; they do not even know what action to take. Insecurity and fear stop them from remediating their situation.

I am not a lawyer. And not everyone understands law. That is why many people seek clarity through the services of attorneys. If you don't know your rights, you become a victim of exploitation. You have every reason to seek the lawyers' services. However, as a father letting his son know essential laws that protect him, I have taken the facts word for word from the New Zealand Government website.

Here are some sections of the Employment Relations Act that might be helpful to know. You can look up the acts on the government website or ring the Human Rights Commission, who will give you advice for free if you think your rights are getting trampled on in your working world. Most countries have laws protecting workers and employers; if yours do not, champion the law enacted.

109 Racial harassment

For the purposes of sections 103(1)(e) and 123(d), an employee is **racially harassed in the employee's employment** if the employee's employer or a representative of that employer uses language (whether written or spoken), or visual material, or physical behaviour that directly or indirectly—
(a) expresses hostility against, or brings into contempt or ridicule, the employee on the ground of the race, colour, or ethnic or national origins of the employee; and

(b) is hurtful or offensive to the employee (whether or not that is conveyed to the employer or representative); and

(c) has, either by nature or through repetition, a detrimental effect on the employee's employment, performance, or job satisfaction.

108 Sexual harassment

(1) For the purposes of sections 103(1)(d) and 123(d), an employee is **sexually harassed in that employee's employment** if that employee's employer or a representative of that employer—

(a) directly or indirectly makes a request of that employee for sexual intercourse, sexual contact, or other forms of sexual activity that contains—
  (i) an implied or overt promise of preferential treatment in that employee's employment; or
  (ii) an implied or overt threat of detrimental treatment in that employee's employment; or
  (iii) an implied or overt threat about the present or future employment status of that employee; or

(b) by—
  (i) the use of language (whether written or spoken) of a sexual nature; or
  (ii) the use of visual material of a sexual nature; or
  (iii) physical behaviour of a sexual nature—
  directly or indirectly subjects the employee to behaviour that is unwelcome or offensive to that employee (whether or not that is conveyed to the employer or representative) and that, either by its nature or through repetition, has a detrimental effect on that employee's employment, job performance, or job satisfaction.

(2) For the purposes of sections 103(1)(d) and 123(d), an employee is also sexually harassed in that employee's employment (whether by a co-employee or by a client or customer of the employer), if the circumstances described in section 117 have occurred.

104 Discrimination

(1) For the purposes of section 103(1)(c), an employee is **discriminated against in that employee's employment** if the employee's employer or a representative of that employer, by reason directly or indirectly of any of the prohibited grounds of discrimination specified in section 105, or the employee's union membership status or involvement in union activities in terms of section 107,—

(a) refuses or omits to offer or afford to that employee the exact terms of employment, conditions of work, fringe benefits, or opportunities for training, promotion, and transfer as are made available for other employees of the same or substantially similar qualifications, experience, or skills employed in the same or substantially similar circumstances; or

(b) dismisses that employee or subjects that employee to any detriment, in circumstances in which other employees employed by that employer on work of that description are not or would not be dismissed or subjected to such detriment; or

(c) retires that employee or requires or causes that employee to retire or resign.

(2) For this section, **detriment** includes anything that has a detrimental effect on the employee's employment, performance, or job satisfaction.

(3) This section is subject to exceptions set out in section 106.

105 Prohibited grounds of discrimination for purposes of section 104

(1) The prohibited grounds of discrimination referred to in section 104 are the prohibited grounds of discrimination set out in section 21(1) of the Human Rights Act 1993, namely—
(a) sex:
(b) marital status:
(c) religious belief:
(d) ethical belief:
(e) colour:
(f) race:
(g) ethnic or national origins:
(h) disability:
(i) age:
(j) political opinion:
(k) employment status:
(l) family status:
(m) sexual orientation.
(2) The items listed in subsection (1) have the meanings (if any) given to them by section 21(1) of the Human Rights Act 1993.

Junior listened intently as I explained the acts, and we went through them together on the website. Then he asked: You explained all these acts, and it is clear what you went through was not right. How do you feel now, Dad?

Life is too short to keep thinking of the past; we have no control of the past, but the future is ours to shape, and the current moment is for us to live in and enjoy. The pain I was carrying every day was only being felt by me, as pain from resentment cannot be shared but only continue to harm yourself, as the other person has no slightest idea of what you are going through. At some point, I felt angry with myself for letting someone hurt me for being vulnerable, but like I said, Son, every adversity brings an opportunity for us to improve and be better people. There were times when every episode came back, and I would start replaying it in my mind. But I would distract myself by thinking of a brighter future without these people in my circle.

Remember those long runs I used to do with Donovan, three times a week, clocking thirty-five kilometres, week in and week out, and the long workouts in the garage? Those were coping mechanisms that worked well for me. They helped clear my mind of any negative thoughts and experiences. But, of course, not everyone recovering from bullying or victimisation should run thirty-five kilometres every week. Still, whatever you can use to distract yourself from replaying the incidents in your mind will help. I also believe that time is a good healer. Bit by bit, the resentment fades away like footprints in the desert. If you don't keep revisiting the thoughts. Muddy water is best cleared by letting it settle. Letting go means being true to yourself, forgiving, and forgetting.

However, only partially letting go does not alleviate the suffering; rather, it exacerbates the pain. More so if you have been living with the pain for some time. The longer you live with pain, the more harm it does to your body. A 2019 study in the *Psychology and Health* journal called 'Meta-analytic connections between forgiveness and health' by Rasmussen and others has shown an association between chronic resentment and health problems, including high blood pressure, migraines, and heart and circulatory problems like stroke. So, you see why we need to let go of any ill feelings we hold against others despite being 'correct'. From a learning perspective, as the wronged person, you need to reflect, introspect and look in your life for patterns that attract what affects you. You might have had long-held beliefs, whatever they may be, like 'bosses are hard to please and are critical'. Consciously or unconsciously, you may exhibit the exact same behaviours towards others—to your subordinates, your son, your daughter or your neighbours.

We are in this plane of life to learn and prepare for higher roles, which should always be our comforting cushion, knowing that you have a brighter, better future without a similar challenge. It would be best to pull the power and strength to overcome whatever challenge is thrown your way out of your reserves.

In retrospect, I have dealt with multiple similar incidences with positive outcomes. One such incident occurred a couple of months after being promoted to a different department. The task I was doing required consulting with a colleague, Sam, so I went on to ask a question in a normal, polite way. Unfortunately, Sam answered me with the 'F' word out of context, so I asked him if he needed to use the 'F' word in his reply, and he repeated the exact phrase. So, I went back to my office and wrote him an email describing what he had said and done, reminding him that the company policy did not allow such behaviour on the premises, and that I do not permit anyone to treat me that way. I copied in his boss, my boss, the Health and Safety Manager, and the HR Manager. The bullying culture was a cancer everyone spoke about but no one did anything about it. I had suffered in a way I did not wish to face again.

The HR Manager had just joined the organisation, and it was probably one of the first cases she had to tackle. She quickly replied to my email the same day and set a date to resolve the matter within two days. On the day of the hearing, she assigned the case to our overall manager. She said the case was the Plant Manager's to resolve, and she would intervene should the matter remain unresolved. Everyone in that meeting had read the email I had sent, so I repeated what had aggrieved me. Sam had no leg to stand on; he knew what he had said and how it was wrong. Even though it was common among the group in that meeting to swear like Sam had done, leadership could not dismiss it, as the company had set up policies to deal with such behaviour. Swearing was no longer acceptable, to someone familiar or not. He got asked to apologise, and the Plant Manager asked Sam and me to have a cuppa together in the cafeteria. We did not have tea together, but Sam changed his behaviour for the better. Soon after that incident, the company, an American multinational corporation, sent the head of employment relations to conduct face-to-face training at the factory. Although most incidences went unreported since most staff did not have the same training and understanding, it became evident that the business was committed to altering the culture.

The behaviour of organisations is set at the top and will cascade to the shop floor. When someone down the chain makes a formal complaint, whoever the objection gets raised against cannot use the defence of 'that's how things get done here'. If it is unethical, no one would support you, and this is the situation in which Sam found himself entangled. Over the years, Sam and I have had friendly chats and developed a good working relationship. Mutual respect was borne out of misaligned beliefs and culture.

The more knowledgeable you are, the fewer people take advantage of you, which also applies to society; the less knowledge the community has, the less it develops and the more human rights abuses there are in that society.

Chapter 5

One O'clock Meetings

One of the meetings I attended representing my department was the one o'clock meeting. All departments involved with product change plans would meet and discuss job preparation progress for the following day or week, and Marcus, my former supervisor, presided over these sessions. Everyone who came to these meetings saw how negatively my contributions were addressed when I raised an issue or something that needed time adjustment. Vinny was one of the managers who went to these meetings, and one day he came in a few minutes late. There was a vacant chair next to me; he sat down and whispered, 'Have they abused you yet?'

I was still awaiting my turn to update the team. When my turn came to update the meeting on how my department was progressing with job preparations, I said my team was going well but would require a couple more hours to complete the task to the expected specifications before a total product change. My comments were quite a norm across departments, as meetings were predicated on perfecting the ancillary tools before changing products, and I was not the first to raise such an issue.

Like Vinny expected, Marcus lashed out at me and told me to quit and find another job elsewhere if the task was not completed within the time limit; no one responded or said anything in that meeting. Only heads bowed down. The belittling was ever-present and evident. The humiliation thrown at me was known to everyone who attended these meetings, but no one raised an alarm other than whisperings. It was quite a way of announcing that he did not want me in these meetings and baiting others to follow suit.

After that meeting, I went back to my department and told my manager what had happened, and I told him I was not going to attend those meetings again, to which he agreed and said he would instead go himself.

A few years later, in my new role, Vinny walked by my office, made some sarcastic jokes and comments, and walked away. Vinny is a heavily built man, with an imposing figure, a gentle giant; many people laughed at his jokes, which I did until I became the butt of his jokes. I did not respond to him, but he made another sarcastic comment when I was in his office with three other staff. I walked away and rang him to say I wanted to talk with him. Vinny came down to my office: only the two of us with no audience for him. His son went to the same school as you, Junior, Sacred Heart, so I said, 'You are aware that what you are doing is not even allowed at the school where our sons go, you realise that...' and before I finished, he apologised and said he was sorry and would not repeat it.

Since that day, Vinny never made fun of me, not in my presence.

Being assertive is a critical trait that you need to display, as people can trample all over you. You have the advantage that you grew up in this country; however, you might still become a target if you are perceived as weak.

Do not be the butt of anyone's joke, as you might be labelled an overall joke and not be taken seriously.

Chapter 6

Baton Passing

The most valuable legacy a generation can leave is knowledge and wisdom for the next. Knowledge and understanding further improve and benefit that generation and those that follow. Your thinking should not reflect my or my dad's thinking but should be a multiplication of past generations' thoughts condensed and improved with your own to create a better world for your kids and grandkids. My dad's parenting skills reflected his dad's skills, which he described as harsh and toughening.

I grew up in a different setup than my dad. But often, he would incorporate and instil those rigid teachings in me, his firstborn; mostly, it revolved around physical toughness, waking up early, not showing signs of weakness or emotions even when you were sick, completing tasks, and so on. These skills were necessary to survive in the savannah or jungle and passed from one generation to another. However, that wisdom must transcend and transform into modern survival skills for the financial jungle. The hunting, gathering and rearing skills are now finance-focused.

Entrepreneurial skills never got passed down in my clan. Maybe they died a stillbirth before reaching my generation or were unnecessary for survival in the savannah. Working for an organisation, for someone or for the government does not give much yield, only enough for having a comfortable lifestyle or survival, depending on the type of work. Suppose you want to make a difference in the world at a higher level. You need to have entrepreneurial skills, as this gives you enough yield and improves your community and society, at your discretion. Working as an employee, you pay taxes that go on to improve the country, yes, but you don't have control over where you want your tax used, unlike a philanthropist, who directs and nominates areas of need. I know I have been telling you about the work environment and my work experiences, which I will keep sharing until the end of the weekend, giving you a perspective on work-life challenges.

I know there are places you can get entrepreneurial skills, like universities and business schools. Still, you will be at an advantage if you know the direction you want to take from an early age and grow up with exposure to business dealings. When you look at people who start businesses, you will see some common elements like businesses being passed on from generation to generation, or monetary inadequacies growing up, coupled with a desire to improve society, the desire to succeed, make money, and enhance the community by addressing a known need, and the desire to ease humanity's challenges.

Why people start businesses:
1. The business is passed on from generation to generation.
2. The experience of monetary inadequacies growing up, coupled with a desire to improve society.
3. The desire to succeed, make money and enhance the community by addressing a known need.
4. The desire to ease humanity's challenges.

My thoughts have been and will always be that every generation needs to improve on the last.

Challenges and difficulties will undoubtedly make their way onto your path. However, here is when you should revert and use the greatest weapon in your arsenal to solve the problem: your knowledge base. Having an armoury, a knowledge base you can refer to for solutions, makes light work of life's challenges.

What I am trying to add to your armoury is what you might need now or in the foreseeable future.

Many people relate to either one of the four elements that I've mentioned are behind great businesses. Still, they choose one that is not among those four, which seems easy based on the knowledge and wisdom that came from previous generations or what governments and society dictate. However, the choice that to many of us looks easy is the most challenging choice of all, and many of us take it unknowingly or due to limitations we have set on ourselves: becoming an employee.

It takes a bit more creativity to improve your yield so that it's more than just enough, which is ok; some might say all I want is enough to live comfortably, but the question is for how long? For one week? For a fortnight? Or for a month? For year? How many years?

As a worker, regardless of your job title, you get paid based on the scarcity of your knowledge, skills and abilities. The pay is a fraction of what the business or organisation makes from your contribution. Of course, there is profit sharing and all the other benefits, but overall, you are limited in what you can earn, which is why it is vital to set up your own business or co-own. You pocket what you are contributing to your business as the owner. You enjoy the full benefits of the effort you invest and get rewarded for the risks you take.

The easy path most people are funnelled into, of being an employee, has lower risk exposure, hence the low yield.

A while ago, one of my co-workers, Nixon, clocked fifty years of continuous service. He witnessed many changes in his fifty years working for the organisation: ownership and leadership changes, growth and decline. However, during the lean periods, there was no week that Nixon did not receive his wages, which is one of the many reasons that kept him loyal to the organisation and probably matched what Nixon set out to achieve. At his commemoration, we all congratulated him for the services he provided to the organisation. He received a certificate as a token of appreciation. Not taking anything away from him or anyone who has committed long service to an organisation, it will be unattainable in the future to have employees clocking fifty years in an organisation unless they co-own.

When you have stock shares, you cease to be just an employee. You get a percentage of the profits through dividends. If you wish to follow in Nixon's footsteps and become a worker, get a job with a publicly listed firm and deposit a portion of each paycheque into the company's stock. After fifty years of service, you'll have a pleasant and significant investment portfolio on top of your superannuation sum. The vital aspect is to continue seeking financial advice to guide you. Mind you, this would be aside from your pension contribution.

Every worker works with a purpose, and purposes vary, but your purpose should not be just survival until your working life expires and you retire and wait for the next life.

When I started investing in the share market, I attended every shareholder's meeting for local stocks; it was thrilling to be at these hotels and convention centres. I would go with a shareholder's invitation letter, sign in, and select a position in the front or second row. I would do a quick scan around and would notice ninety percent of the shareholders were grey-haired and probably retired, and I was the only one like me. I would get curious gazes and some odd ones, too; some shareholders would come and chat with me after the presentation. In most of these presentations, I would meet familiar faces; we were probably using the same financial advisor, or the stocks we had were the most attractive ones. I was targeting the more stable ones, which paid dividends, as it was part of testing the waters.

Fisher and Paykel Healthcare (FPH) gave one such investor presentation I attended at the Ellerslie Convention Centre. The new CEO had just taken over. The way he assured the shareholders that their money was safe was quite impressive. How he set his targets of doubling the company market value every five years and showed where the market was and how it was growing was phenomenal. Five years later, the share price tripled, surpassing what he had said, thanks to Covid-19.

I thought and wondered what it would be like to work for such an organisation, what culture was in the organisation, how were the employees treated, what got valued in the operations, and what were the steps in their processes?

If you ask any company representative such questions at an event like this or any other occasion, rest assured that they will paint a glowing picture. As I said, the desire to understand and experience different company cultures grew in me after my experiences at my parent company. Though my experiences had tainted my expectations overall, it was a good company with some bad apples. For that reason, I did not want to quit, since I knew unethical behaviour would be unsustainable, and goodwill eventually outshines the bad.

After my brief stint in the courier company, I thought it would be a blessing to have insight and inside experience in FPH.

My good friend Jolene, whom I had worked with at the fries-making factory, had a job at FPH and knew I enjoyed working side jobs. She told me there were openings at the company. I could join if I wanted; all I had to do was submit my application through a link. She also gave me the details of the contact person I had to call.

Hooray! My puzzle pieces were coming together, I thought to myself. This assignment would be the last of my fact-finding missions, and I was looking forward to making the most of it. It would not be a challenge regarding the long hours I was to work. I had done it before at the fries-making factory.

I had psyched myself for the challenge.

Over the phone, Roxana, the contact person, had said that since I had a full-time job elsewhere, I might not be able to cope, but I convinced her I had done it before, so I was ready for it. I gave her Ho's number, a shift manager from the fries factory, as my reference, who gave her a glowing reference. She invited me for an interview, a raft of psychometric tests that took about four hours. I was to be contacted within three days.

Three days passed, and I didn't get a call. Never did I ever doubt that I would miss out on this mission. They told me to be patient, and within a week, I was contacted and offered a six-month contract, which was the maximum they could give me, and it was more than enough for what I wanted to achieve. I was assigned to work in the warehouse as a store's afternoon shift person from 4 pm to midnight. My day job was from 7 am to 3:30 pm. I took a test drive between the two workplaces to ascertain the drive time. Fifteen minutes. Great! I thought. I told myself that I could even knock off ten minutes late from my day job and would still be able to get to my new job on time with regular traffic. I had to schedule my work to avoid overlapping the two assignments with these timelines.

A verse from the Bible came to my mind that says, 'No man can serve two masters: either he will hate the one and love the other;

or else he will hold to the one, and despise the other.' (Matthew 6:24, King James Version). My case was not about splitting my 'love' but meeting my obligations to both, without one affecting the other.

Chapter 7

Best in Class

Growing up, never in my dreams did I ever think that I would be working two or three jobs at some point in my life. I saw no reason to be overworking oneself like that. I assumed that the human body needs to sleep eight to nine hours uninterrupted, which is the standard recommendation. But somewhere along the lines, I thought of hunters and gatherers in ancient times that if they had to sleep those eight uninterrupted hours in the savanna, they would have been extinct, with all the animals that hunted at night, like hyenas, jackals and lions.

I came across a 2015 study on the world's last surviving hunter-gatherer populations by Gandhi Yetish and others. These are the San of Namibia, the Hadza of Tanzania, and Tsimané of Bolivia.

Cut off from electricity, social media, TV and everything modern, the premise was that these hunter-gatherers exhibited the same sort of natural sleep humans enjoyed 10,000 years ago. The study found 'a striking uniformity in their sleep patterns despite their geographic isolation. On average, all three groups sleep less than 6.5 hours a night, do not take naps, or go to sleep when it gets dark' (*Washington Post*, 2015).

If these guys were sleeping 6.5 hours on average a night without any health issues and not sleeping as comfortably as I did in my comfy bed, I could do five hours, which I used to sleep when I studied. It was more than ten years ago, but I saw no reason

I couldn't do it now. So, it was not hard for me to turn into a short-sleeper.

I started my second job two days before the first Covid-19 lockdown. Because of the looming health disaster, demand for FPH products soared. There was no better time to learn how companies like FPH would cope within their processes to meet customer deadlines and support their values and beliefs, which are customer- and employee-centric. HR told me I had been recruited because of the looming Covid-19 pandemic.

The induction took a whole day, from 8 am to 3 pm. So, I took a day off from my day job to attend. The team that took us through the induction modules was diverse, helpful and friendly. Before the end of the day, I was introduced to my afternoon team, a small team I thought, only four guys, including the supervisor.

Many of us make assumptions and prejudge when we meet new people, especially those with whom we share a chunk of our time. However, unconscious biases get peeled off as we get to know the individuals more. Some keep those biases despite getting to know the person, which is not something you should worry about, Son, as what people think of you is theirs to ponder. All you need to display is your true personality; it is easier to be yourself than pretend to be someone else. Your true nature will always reveal itself regardless of your effort to conceal it.

I noted my work history in my resumé, and the HR team knew I had a full-time day role elsewhere. I planned not to let anyone in the team know about my full-time position, a lesson I had learned from the fries factory. Instead, I intended to gain unbiased work experience information from my team and everyone on the shop floor not knowing about my other job. In the introductions, I told everyone that I had moved from the fries factory, which was up the road, and about all the other places I had worked, except my full-time job.

During the first week, I was trained on how the company's just-in-time delivery process worked. The production team pulled parts through a resource planning ticketing system in SAP every fifteen minutes.

My role was to pick machine parts from bin locations in the warehouse and deliver them to production bin locations with a delivery tow truck within the factory, which allowed me to talk to most people on the afternoon shift. I believed my day job company was a large organisation until I got to FPH, which had more than two thousand employees. The afternoon crew had more than five hundred personnel of diverse ethnic backgrounds: Sāmoans, Tongans, Cook Islanders, Indians, Chinese, Vietnamese, Mexicans, Brazilians, Spanish, Filipinos, South Africans, Pākehā, Māori, Zimbabweans, and more. The diversity was reflected in my warehouse crew; of the five of us, four came from different countries.

My supervisor was one of the most pleasant individuals I had ever met. From the first day, I noticed his genuineness in training me, as he brought me up to speed with the delivery times. Warehouse performance was measured by how parts got delivered within one hour, from the pull order time to the time the machine part was scanned into its destination bin. The frequency at which wrong parts were delivered to production areas or errors made in inward goods receipts was also monitored.

The production team had targets of producing a given set of units per shift, and if they reached the mark, they would get different incentives like canteen vouchers or knocking off early.

I did not get to meet my manager until the third day. Before starting the shift, my team met to discuss task allocation and the previous day's performance review, which had a graph—and a motivational, encouraging and praising talk was given.

Rod, the manager, joined us at my third meeting. He waited until the supervisor had finished his part and then gave his pep talk. He talked about how the production team planned to ramp up production to meet a rise in demand. Our staff had to increase by three more to take the total to eight. His demeanour mirrored the CEO's investor presentation I had witnessed a few years back. Respect for one another was always at the forefront.

I saw the cascading of expected behaviours from the top to the shop floor. I had only been three days in the factory, but I was already beginning to feel like I had been working there for an eternity. Everyone was friendly, and it was as if they had been waiting for me all along. My friend Jolene also worked the afternoon shift in another building. I did not get to see her until after a week. My mission was to get as much insight into the organisation as possible; I asked her how she was enjoying the workplace, and she said the place was way better in all disciplines than the fries-making factory.

First and foremost, she liked the money she was getting paid. She had been working a lot of overtime since joining the company and was not complaining as the money was good. Her team was good, her bosses were good, and the food in the canteen was good and well-subsidised. She was undergoing training for a new role. Her team had a rotating system, so employees could not get quality fatigue from repeatedly doing the same task as was the case in the fries factory. The rotating pattern kept them focused, interested and motivated; and, to top it off, she had a good boss, which was a recipe for the best workplace for any would-be employee.

I concurred with everything she said about the company; even though I was a newbie, I had been welcomed and greeted with a warm smile everywhere I went within the company. The environment made employees feel good about themselves, translating to good results, regardless of their assigned tasks.

****

I always try to have one comprehensive plan for whatever I do. However, that does not mean that the goal will be achieved. Still, it means there is no need to put effort into preparing for failure with Plan B, Plan C, Plan D, and so on in queue; these contingency plans only mean that you are acknowledging that you have not done all that is necessary and required to achieve Plan A. Contingent Plans B, C, and so on should be other plans for a new project. For example, there has been significant interest in going to space over the last few years. And when the planning is underway, all the effort is put into ensuring that the rocket will achieve the purpose of its design when it launches into space; no Rocket B will be waiting on the launchpad next to Rocket A, to take its place. All the resources get canvassed to make sure the rocket will launch. When the rocket fails to achieve the desired goal, a new plan gets created with previously failed learnings incorporated into it. Edison failed one thousand times before he succeeded at inventing the lightbulb.

Such is the way I took my second job. I made sure that I brought my all to the role.

Being introverted has its advantages and disadvantages; the less I talked about myself, the less interested the team became in my background.

Sometimes, however, the macho in us overpowers the self-control we set ourselves up with, especially when there are adoring women around who want to know more about us. But, looking back, I managed to do a perfect job of concealing my identity until the last day of my afternoon shift, apart from not working overtime.

I made sure that I showed no interest in staying back except on some Fridays and later some weekends. Nobody bothered to ask me why I was not particularly eager to work overtime when everyone was keen on increasing their paycheque through overtime.

Three months down my contract, our staff complement had grown to eight. The new guys were out to prove that they could work as many hours of overtime as the supervisor could give them. One day, Jak, my coworker, said something in passing about my not working overtime, and I said, 'Let Jay have it; he is still young and has a young family; he needs the money more than I do,' which was true in every sense.

My supervisor, Mohan, encouraged me to apply and become a permanent employee as there were some vacancies two months into my contract. I made the excuse that I needed to complete some assignments before getting a permanent role at FPH. He knew my employment contract would be terminated after six months and was keen to have me become permanent. Personnel development was at the core of FPH. Leaders were measured and reviewed on the effectiveness of their training to subordinates. One interesting weekly graph on our department notice board was the worker satisfaction report, which was intimated by the absenteeism record.

None of the companies I had worked for or been to had any form of employee satisfaction measure, let alone weekly, and displayed for employees and bosses to see the effectiveness of their leadership styles. The graph reminded me of my incident with Hertha and how I had decided not to turn up for the shift after being upset.

One of the organisation's core values was that its strength revolved around its people, so they said. I was witnessing that belief. By focusing on employee happiness, the company was reaping rewards in high productivity.

No matter how I phrased my informal questions to my colleagues, the answer was always positive toward the company. In rare cases, I would get the 'Oh, I am so tired' responses, followed by, 'but I am all good.' The prevailing positive attitude overrode the fatigue.

I also met Alex, who was Zimbabwean. His situation had been

kind of tragic. He was an airline pilot who had been laid off due to Covid-19. He had migrated two years earlier than I had. Life had been excellent, 'living the dream', as he liked to call it. He had been to all corners of the world, had seen it all and had opted to settle here, a great choice, he said, to which I always concurred. We were of the same age and had experienced the early phase of life in our mother countries, with the good and the deteriorating parts, which eventually led us each to desert our nation for this one.

His airline was unsure when he would be recalled, just like all businesses affected by Covid-19 travel restrictions. He had decided to come and work for FPH, as it gave him the necessary money to pay part of his mortgage. He was one of the few outside my department who I told about my full-time role elsewhere. Knowing how hardworking our lot can be, it did not surprise him much.

It was quite a transition for him from captaining a Boeing 707 to working on a production line assembling respirators and inhalers. On Mondays, he would say, 'It feels like I never had a weekend. I am still tired from last week,' to which I would say, 'Same here.'

Despite the change in circumstances, he was happy to be doing his work at FPH. The ability to integrate people from higher roles into lesser roles and have them still feel good about themselves was one stand-out point I gave to the FPH organisation. He was one of many pilots laid off due to Covid-19 who had decided to look for employment in other sectors prospering from the pandemic.

Regardless of the challenge you face, Son, if you look hard enough, an opportunity will be waiting for you somewhere that will at least keep you going even if it is not the right one for you. The ideas that you generate in your mind will always materialise if you do not lose sight of what you desire to achieve. Your thinking leads you to wherever you are in life over time. Not everyone is where they are because of their thinking, but their thinking would have put them in that position if they had chosen to remain there.

Never should your ideas be affected by fear of being judged by family, friends, relatives, neighbours or society. That fear, self-doubt or inferiority mindset takes nobody anywhere—it keeps you in the same position. Therefore, moving from any situation to the next in your life depends on how you conquer that fear of failure and inferiority complex.

Alex told me he grew up on a farm working the land, so putting in the extra effort was not an issue. He could have chosen to remain at home, getting the government unemployment benefit like some were doing, but that dependency syndrome was not in him, so he said.

When I delivered parts to his department one afternoon, he told me he was interested in swapping to the warehouse and asked if I knew the requirements, qualifications or experience for him to get considered for a position, should it arise. I told him I was unsure what they had considered when employing me. See, in my case, I did not apply for a specific position. I thought I would end up in the assembly department like most people who were employed at that time. When I spoke to Roxana before submitting my resumé at FPH, she had told me the HR department would place me in a role that matched my previous experience and qualifications, which I told Alex. I advised him to speak to Roxana about that, as she was accommodating and friendly.

The following day, he waved at me as I drove towards his section on the delivery tow truck. We had to beep the tow truck horn every time we got to a blind corner. And every time you entered or exited a building, production staff would know you were coming in advance. The tow truck was on its way in his direction; Alex was waiting for me to share what Roxana had told him about the job requirements of a storeperson. Roxana had asked if he held a fork hoist license, and he did not have one. I then remembered that I had a fork hoist license, which I seldom used at my primary job. I had kept renewing it every time it expired, and finally, it had found its purpose of helping me land a role in FPH stores.

Alex told Roxana that it would not be a challenge for him to drive a fork hoist as his job was to fly Boeing 707s, which are way more complicated than a fork hoist. We both laughed at the differences in the machines. He told me he would arrange for the fork hoist training in the coming weeks.

As I drove back to the warehouse, I replayed what Alex had said about flying a Boeing 707 and now being asked for a fork hoist license. I thought, *What a switch*. However, I admired his willingness to step off the Boeing 707 and sit on a fork hoist just because he wanted to do it. Alex was not worried about negative opinions from former workmates, family or society. He was concerned about getting the fork hoist licence, as it had more value at that moment than the Boeing 707 pilot licence.

Picking up a new skill, a new source of income or a new qualification should not be based on the qualifications or experience you already have but on what you want to achieve at that moment in time. Achieving that desired outcome should be what matters to you.

It would be best if you were like an eagle, Son, flying high up, alone. When there are obstacles of small birds around that distract, hinder your vision or increase the alertness of your prey, remain focused on your target but move away from them. The higher you fly away from the small birds, the more you will mix and mingle with those who share your vision and help you strategise your attack and the kill on the ground.

Collaborate with those who value you and vice versa. However, you should always note that every individual has value and should be treated with equal respect, but those who are on the same wavelength are the ones you should seek to establish a collaborative bond with. You can identify them by their willingness to help you grow, to be influenced by you, spend time with you and take on your way of thinking, but also by your own willingness to do the same for them.

> People to collaborate with can be identified by a mutual willingness to:
> – Help each other grow
> – Be influenced by each other
> – Spend time with each other
> – Listen to one another
> – Accept each other's thinking
> – Merge thinking

A few years ago, I was in a WhatsApp group called 'Boys', which comprised people who had migrated into this country around the same time. We gathered every Saturday and mixed with the broader community for a soccer game, usually from four to six in the evening. After that, we would have a barbeque and social drinks, and exchange views on various matters. We used to discuss challenges that we were facing in our jobs, businesses and studies. During the week, we would be sharing stories and general opinions on pretty much everything, then we would discuss at large on Saturday by the barbeque. Some personalities are not meant to be in groups or to collaborate; the emotionally insecure ones always reject other people's ideas and do not contribute anything meaningful. As the years passed by and people got accustomed to their new country and gained citizenship, many emigrated again and crossed the ditch. The statistics show that it is more financially lucrative across the trench in Australia than in New Zealand.

The WhatsApp group had more than twenty members initially, and one after another, members started exiting; then, one day, I decided to leave, too. When you are not benefiting or developing mentally from a group, there is no need to hang around. You will be flying with small birds that will cause you to fail to reach the heights you have set yourself to achieve.

Talking of migrating after emigrating is a phenomenon that can happen when you get to a new place and the life you'd aimed for still looks distant. The target keeps getting further and further away, even though the effort you exert should create double the reward in a country with a shortage of the skills you possess. This is the situation some of my colleagues faced. I entertained the thoughts of emigrating, too, for a while. But the desire was not as much as when I moved here.

We managed to buy a house and then a rental property quickly. So, the thoughts and enticement were not as alluring to me as someone struggling to get on to the property market. 'Lucky' for us. No—no such thing as luck; remember I spoke about this earlier. It is setting your priorities right. If you want a statement that describes our position at that time, well...

When I entertained the thoughts of crossing the ditch, remember your friends Tino, Vimbai, and their families invited you to visit them across the trench for the holidays after their move? Their parents talked much about the financial progress they had made shortly after migrating. You liked the place and came back with stories of all the places you had visited, malls, amusement parks and the zoo. I reminded you that we have the same here, too, though not at the same scale.

I took a three-week vacation to visit all the cities my colleagues had relocated to, to weigh the benefits of moving versus remaining in this country. Remember I told you a while ago that I grew up in a city and have always enjoyed city life? However, I found out that the money that had enticed many of my colleagues to move over was in the mines, where you would have to fly to the mine, spend some days or weeks there without family, then fly back to the city for your off days. I did not find that attractive enough. Also, living in a mine was unappealing after listening to some of the stories about mental health issues. I found that the jobs in the city that were like my job over here would not have made much difference to our lifestyle. And that is why I decided to stay here and enjoy the peace and protection from the government against world pandemics.

****

I know most of your friends that you have grown up with and not many of the ones you have made in the last couple of years, and those are the ones I worry about, as friends can have a positive or negative influence depending on your emotional stability. I have always said no one should influence your decisions but yourself. Remember the night we were watching TV—we had just finished watching a movie and were flicking across the recently added movies on Netflix so we could view another one together, father and son, then, *Ping!* Your phone went off. The next minute you were saying you were going out. Your friend had texted you, and I noted: 'Son, you are getting influenced here. Your plans for the night were to relax and watch Netflix with Dad; a text from a friend cannot quickly change that.' It was an example of how you needed to be firm in your social or business decision-making. When you have put effort into planning, changing that plan should not be instant, a flick of a button because someone wants their priorities met over yours. Steadfastness can be one success key for you.

For every challenge you encounter, remember I have faced it in a different setting. My settings would probably have been more complex than yours. If you have a situation where you have reached the end of your thinking capacity, always remember that your dad has faced a similar problem. As your dad, I am in this universe to pass my learnings to you and the next generation. Success in this relationship, which leads to other successes, is achieved when you and I are happy to interact in whatever we do without any resentment. You are taking my advice to build on your knowledge for your children and generations after that. You will, however, pretty much follow the same circle as you build your wisdom, as the seasons follow each other every year.

You, like everyone else, collect data along the way from all life's experiences: in your neighbourhood, school, college and university, in the workplace, in church, at bars, at the sports field, from friends. Even from those who do not have much affinity for you. You will then process that data into information that helps guide, direct and progress you in similar circumstances in the future. In the same vein, you turn that information into knowledge that you will pass on to those who did not have similar experiences but need your guidance to progress more quickly toward *their* desired goals, as I am doing to you now.

You might not remember everything I am telling you now, but when you get to a situation requiring the knowledge I have passed to you, that knowledge will spring out and help propel you to the next step. Then the more years you live in this universe, the more you turn that knowledge into wisdom, and new generations will come to you for advice as you will be the trusted elder, based on how rich your life has been, not financially, but rich in how you have amassed life's experiences through challenges and successes. If you look in any community you will surely know of the elders I am talking about, those who get consulted when everyone has reached the end of their thinking capacity. They are referred to as the 'whiteheads' because of their grey hair and the wisdom they've brought from the history and circumstances we all come from.

If you look at the societies that are prospering, you will notice the community always enjoys a harmonious relationship. Common elements bind the society together. The moment negativity flows in the community, the less development happens. The universe has rules we humans need to follow to achieve whatever we, as individuals or as a collective, want.

You will notice as you mature that there are some situations where you keep getting the same results despite changing the situation. It might be a job, relationship or financial matter. You keep attracting the same issues. The point is that you cannot run away from your problems in this universe. Even migrating would not resolve your issues entirely until you have learned what the universe is teaching you. I know of a friend who entered this country hoping that a different environment would resolve his marital problems. The couple talked candidly with each other that whatever differences they had back in their country causing them to have an unhappy marriage should be forgotten and that they would start a new slate altogether.

They did live in a temporarily collaborative marriage for the first couple of years as they only had each other for support. They both went out of their way to ensure they transitioned well into their new life. But the talk they had had of forgiving and forgetting got eroded somewhere along the line; they had both packed their emotional baggage and brought it over instead of resolving the issues back home at the source.

The resentment had been lodged and hidden in the abyss of their subconscious minds those first couple of years but was ratcheting out slowly, year after year. Every incident in those unhappy years back in their country was resurrected, re-lived and referred to with every argument and incident that ensued. They watered and fed the seeds of past unhappiness. Their quarrels became increasingly frequent over the past, until they could no longer live with each other any more in the present. The past came to be the present again. Whether they had resolved their differences here or in their country, their problems persisted and followed them. The universe wanted them to have a good reflection on themselves. The past cannot triumph over the power of the present unless granted permission by you.

You lose access to your money in your bank account when you lose your password. Right? You will only access and withdraw it when you have remembered the password or called the bank to give you access; this is how life works. We're all governed by laws that need to be respected if we want to enjoy what is rightfully ours.

Everything we do impacts us as individuals, either positively or negatively, like the seasons, which occur according to the rules of nature; plants shed their leaves, lambs are born in the spring, and some birds migrate across the world to follow the spring and summer conditions, which are warm and support an insect bounty.

Universal laws guide humans too, nothing escapes the principle of rhythm. Rhythm is more noticeable in our moods, which affect our behaviour, causing it to fluctuate at times without our involvement, from high productive thinking to low; in our health, we reach peak performance and then decline. In all that we do, if we don't maintain a balance in our lifestyle, which helps to lower the effects of rhythm, we remain victims and blame anyone and everyone. But being aware makes us masters who can ride the tide and follow the pattern like migrating birds do. The outcomes depend on our choices as we progress through life. As we grow older and mature, our progress and evolution will be determined by how well we learn, both in the sound and in the challenging times.

How we have learned as individuals or as a society determines how we progress to the next stage. If we have not grasped it, we keep getting the same challenges, albeit in slightly altered forms, ensuring we cannot move to the next step, like contestants on the *Amazing Race*. We pivot, and we progress.

Regardless of religious denomination or spiritual affiliations, atheist or agnostic, the ways and laws that cut across humanity are common, though not familiar to the oblivious ones. If we all knew about them and followed them, the path to the next station of our destination would be much easier and lighter. However, remember that we have free will. That means we can choose what matters most in our current lives. The choices have options, and any alternative you pick will lead you onto the path you have asked for at some point, good or bad. Unfortunately, some choices we make with our available knowledge end up pear-shaped and misaligned with our desires, which can be disheartening and discouraging to most, but not to those who know how the universe functions. To them, this will be like a misplaced cone on the road; you will need to move it to its rightful position, and carry on with your journey.

Every 'because' can be identified, and nothing happens for no reason.

Families, associations, clubs, businesses and political groups all have ways to elicit individuals to have acceptable norms and contributions that benefit the group. The collectiveness in those groups, affiliations and denominations is the same that connects the society, country and the universe at large. We are all interlinked and connected through creation. Every atom inside us links to the rest of the universe we move through. And that means that whatever we give out, bad or good, we get back. Everything you do has a reverse effect that positively or negatively impacts the source of the deed: you. Our acts to others are like boomerangs that curl back to the thrower.

We are bundles of energy; everything in this universe is energy, the clothes you are putting on, the couch you are sitting on, the car you drive, the food you eat, the bed you sleep on. Everything that exists that is seen and unseen, your thoughts are energy, and when there is a change in one part of this energy field, other features are affected too.

Remember, Son, the *divine oneness* in this universe, all the energy in this universe, is linked back to the source, the creator; as you know from your science subjects, energy cannot get destroyed but can only be redirected for other purposes.

> Our acts to others are like boomerangs that curl back to the thrower.

If only everyone in this universe knew the depth of this interconnectedness. How our acts and deeds, good and evil, have a profound impact that alters the state of the universe. We would all be striving to be positive and empathetic to one another—the division mentality imposed and imprinted in our minds by generations gone by would be non-existent. However, there is light at the end of the tunnel for the world to be united again.

Younger generations, you included, Son, are getting less captivated, fascinated and attracted to the past dogmas, the mentality that divides people based on colour, language, tribe, geographic location or origin. This is not to say that those who propagate the division gospel are suddenly going extinct. On the contrary, most hibernate, only coming to lash out when what they stand for is replaced by something else that encompasses and incorporates every soul. However, each new generation is breaking and weakening the conduits that feed generations to come with the narrative of race, colour, origin or superiority to others, which is where the source of human segregation, division and separatism originates.

We sometimes get lost in our selfishness, our egos overtaking our rationalised thinking capabilities until we have lost sight of what caused unwanted circumstances. The lost origin of these circumstances is the challenge that will keep popping up in your life journey until fully corrected. In our egocentrism, we fail to recognise that every word or action we say that hurts another person is pain that gets returned by the universe in some form or another. Any unkind word you say or do to hurt another person hurts yourself. The resentment and anger that boils in you will be creating unwanted chemicals within you that will manifest in some form at some point in your life as a health condition well after your anger subsides.

****

Digressing is in my nature, and I get lost in my thoughts, Son, I said with hearty laughter. I must have picked it up from my granny, who was a great storyteller but always digressed in every story that she told so that she would end up saying, 'Which part did I end up on, by the way, before I started this story?' and everyone would laugh their heads off. Her stories were captivating, but the most fun part was when Grandma forgot her storyline.

Job satisfaction within an individual has many facets, including intrinsic and extrinsic factors. The intrinsic elements need to be identified, taken in, and believed in order to accept and acknowledge the extrinsic factors, the conditions that drive us to achieve the set target and outcome. 'Satisfaction' on its own is just a word with no roots or weight and no impact whatsoever on our emotions. It only becomes a word of note that elicits emotions when we compare it to what we have experienced or perceive as what gives us 'satisfaction' relative to something else.

'What a great working environment,' I would say to myself every time I clocked in for my afternoon shift after my day job. I surprised myself with how energised I became every shift. The warm, friendly smiles were infectious. I would think that this workplace is ideal for fresh graduates or someone getting into the workplace for the first time. But was it the perception I had built before joining the organisation or was it the positivity and camaraderie within my team that drove and cranked up my energy levels on every shift?

Rod, our manager, would make it a point to have a one-on-one conversation with team members. What made Rod connect with most of us, me precisely, was his friendly and genuine approach. He made people feel valued and supported by genuinely being interested in each person's success and personal wellbeing—he also made regular check-ins with the crew about their lives at work and home.

Remember, we were under the first Covid-19 lockdown, and I was an 'essential worker', so I continued working while most had to stay home. My employment in both positions was not affected, unlike most of my friends in the tourism and catering industries. However, it was apparent how extended family, friends and neighbours were being affected by the lockdown, and often, we talked about Covid-19 effects in general. Did I tell you that I felt like I was the missing chip of the colour spectrum when I walked in on the first day? I guessed by its composition that Rod was building a diverse and inclusive team and that he encouraged diversity of thought, based on our daily meetings, in which he encouraged everyone to air their views.

The company developed a gift care-package two months into

the first lockdown. Every worker got a fifty-dollar grocery voucher and a packed gift box with essentials. Unlike my primary employer, the canteen remained open with no service disruption to workers. FPH implemented all the social distancing protocols in the canteen, ensuring workers enjoyed the expected service. I had direct comparisons of how the two companies were handling the pandemic.

At the time FPH made a policy of wearing face masks and issued them for every employee, my day job company and even the country at large did not see the need. Instead, FPH set out essential worker standards that set the tone and soon became mandatory nationwide. One impressive tool they came up with was the traceability cards, a tracker that each worker was issued and had to wear on a lanyard. The chip in the card registered all the co-workers you met at any given time and helped identify close contacts, should anyone develop Covid-19 symptoms or get infected at the workplace.

Their values and beliefs stated that 'We care for our patients, customers, suppliers, shareholders, the environment, and each other.'

I witnessed that what they said, they did. I saw it as a shareholder—the impressive presentations and the equally impressive growth and dividends, which you were assured of reaping as a shareholder. No excuses: the only changes to shareholders were positive gains. I saw it as a shop floor employee: the unquestionable care, no pretence, and the cascading of company values from the top were abundantly clear. The Covid-19 care team was impressive in handling workers who developed symptoms. Do you remember when I developed flu-like symptoms from sanding walls when we renovated our rental property? I rang the team to say, 'I have Covid-19-like symptoms. I know what is causing them; I have been sanding walls and have a dust allergy.' The team asked me a list of questions that did not apply to me. Since I had visited a town where Covid-19 cases were on the rise, the safety team recommended that for the sake of everyone, and to avoid alarming my co-workers, I needed to get tested and stay home until I was clear of any symptoms. They told me they would be checking on my progress through phone calls after a couple of days.

How you care for a sick family member is how the FPH care team cared for me. As a worker, getting that care and commitment from an employer motivates you to contribute your bit with an equally total commitment. It took three days for the Covid-19 test results to come back, and as soon as I got them back, I texted the team my results. The process of coming back from Covid-19 test results was to go to the clinic first, and the nurse would do temperature checks, ensuring you did not display the symptoms that might alarm your co-workers.

At my primary job, I got asked to text my results. If they were negative, of course, I would go on with my work as usual, which is a norm by any means, but if you compare the differences in approaches and care, they were at two ends of a spectrum, and that is where the satisfaction level comes into play.

Our experiences transform and reshape us. Or is it that we change and reshape ourselves based on the knowledge we acquire on life's journey?

Circumstances do not make a person but do reveal them. The revelation comes when you realise that you are a master of yourself. Everyone around you, family, friends, workmates, subordinates, bosses, your girlfriend, husband, wife and neighbours, are only playing the part you asked them to play in your 'play'. Good or bad, you can edit, reshape, and re-cast the actors in your play. It is no Shakespeare, but it is *your* play.

Chapter 8

Self-Meeting

I have meetings with myself often now. I have learned to respect and be patient with myself.

I miss my old self and love my new self and wish my old self could have had the new me to guide him.

Hence, I am discussing with you, Son, that you might use some of my new self in your current self, to make yourself more life-ready than I am when you get to half my current age.

As I went back and forth to my two jobs every day, five days a week, leaving home at six in the morning and coming back at thirty minutes past midnight gave me little time to brood and daydream. I was living in the moment. The mind and body had to work in constant harmony to finish the long day, let alone the weeks, the months and the year.

The plan was to work only for six months and then stick with one typical day job. My employment agent told me I was only allowed to work for six months because of my permanent day job. I gelled so well with my team that my supervisor kept mentioning a permanent role for me when we had general conversations. One thing I have learned over the years and across the places I have worked is to be wary of what you say about work when you are with co-workers. There is always someone who conveys what you say to the next level up or the next group along, be it good or bad.

The likely objective for these individuals is probably some perceived reward that comes with that behaviour. The more insecure they are, the more likely they are to be ingratiating. It is essential to know who that person is when you are a newbie to a workplace, as they will either help your cause or destroy your dreams by passing on whatever you say to someone above them. I did not want to raise everyone's expectation of my becoming permanent, so I said over smoko in passing that I was waiting for something to materialise and was not looking for a permanent role.

My statement did find its way to Mohan, the supervisor, for the second time after telling him myself, but it didn't affect, alter or change the treatment I received from him.

The way we react, emotionalise, and verbalise our responses to a situation mirrors the turmoil inside, awaiting an excuse to vent. Yet, blessed are those with an inner calmness that external surroundings and environment does not affect.

You notice I have changed quite a bit over the years, the way I communicate with you, Son. Speaking styles tend to be passed on from parent to child in most cases. As a child, you may not like the way your parent talks to you when you have erred or generally, but as you mature and have kids, you tend to follow the same pattern that you did not like when you were growing up. You do not need to find justification or reasons for following that path, surprisingly enough. My dad came from a large family, twenty of them. Yes, you heard correctly, Son, twenty kids from the same man and three wives living on the same compound. That probably made it easier to have so many kids, as it was not one house but several. Imagine what sort of personality Granddad had to control such a large family. Patience was one definition indeed that did not exist in daily chores. As a subsistence farmer with a results-driven personality, Granddad was not left with time on his hands; working long hours was the order of the day for my dad and his siblings in their fields.

When my father got together with his family, I would listen to him and his siblings reminiscing and ruminating about their growing-up years. My dad's characterisation of Granddad is how I would have described Dad at the time. If someone had asked me to 'describe' my dad, I would have used the exact terms. What had become embedded in him was a standard way of teaching, guiding and directing his offspring.

Subconsciously I found myself perpetuating the same behaviours I despised in my dad. I have a good relationship with my dad. But I had some resentment growing up; I learned life lessons through those challenging teachings. But after reflection, you realise that there should be better ways of developing, nurturing and building character in your son that do not always involve army-style discipline. Unless one generation breaks the practice, the cycle of passing on these despised ways within the family will continue.

Chapter 9

Son-Dad Wish List

The idea came about while stuck in traffic going to my afternoon job. Some brilliant ideas come about when people are stuck in traffic. Have you ever given a quick scan around when traffic is moving at a snail's pace? How pensive will some drivers be? Of course, there will be those who will be enjoying their playlists at total volume, bursting their eardrums, some listening to talkback radio shows etcetera.

I was one with the reflective look, when the idea flashed in my mind. I thought, how great would it be if I could involve you in my growth? I am grown up in stature but still maturing, yes. I am still increasing in experiences and wisdom, though I'm not physically growing. Change is ongoing till we leave this planet for the next phase. We are all works in progress. A good relationship between son and dad should not have gaps because the common thinking has diverged. As sons grow up, dads nurture their kids' thinking to come up to their own level; however, as the kids pass through different levels of education, their thinking and reasoning capacity will match or probably surpass their dad's thinking, which is the point where the divergence of opinions might occur instead of *convergence* and collaboration. I do not want to be a grumpy older man because we have failed to maintain our bond.

I know you are proud of your dad, the way you speak highly of me to your friends, which you always mention, I said to Junior. It is a blessing to have a son who speaks highly of his dad, and I appreciate that, Son. Anyway, thanks for doing as I suggested and discussing with your friends and writing up your relationship wish list for us or, broadly, 'Sons' expectations of their dads'.

First, let's review your wish list. Should I have my list, too? Nah, just kidding, my list has been a work in progress since you were born, Son.

It's all good, Dad; sons imitate dads and will alter their thinking as they interact more with the world, including with their friends' dads. Junior showed me the list he'd put together.

> Junior's wish list of expectations for his dad:
> 1. General support
> 2. Communication
> 3. Verbal affirming
> 4. Time together
> 5. Personal life experience advice

Thanks for that, Son. We only become aware of our children's wish lists if we ask; it might be awkward for sons to say to dads, here is a list of things you should do to be an ideal dad, out of context. I appreciate the time you have set aside to develop your list. However, I will need your input to understand your list more by asking you questions as we go through the list, I said.

Not a problem, Dad. I will help you to help me, Junior replied.

1. General support
What do you mean, Son, by general support? It is not clear for me or any dad to know what is required of them to give general support. Do you have any specific items you need ticking off? I said.

No, not really, Dad; the specifics are on points two to five. Here, I mean supporting my growth, clothing, food on the table, shelter, education and basic needs. I know you did that and sent me to schools you could afford. But I should mention general support as it is the bedrock of any father-son or father-daughter relationship. I noticed the effort you put into my having a good upbringing, which I will take and do for my kids. You enrolled me in a soccer academy at five years old and took me to my games every Saturday morning. I enjoyed it very much until I decided to change the sport; you accepted my decision even though you were disappointed, but I felt your support everywhere, Junior said.

Yes, Son, that's the role of fathers: it does come naturally to most. The less fathers had in their own childhood, the more they strive to provide what they missed to their children. However, it may depend on the fathers' beliefs and learnings. Some may want to replicate their upbringing and take no effort to improve their offspring's. Most fathers desire to change and improve their children. I know I have said every generation needs to be better than the one before, which I hope is not coming across as overbearing, as resentment gets borne out of it, which can cloud how sons think of their fathers.

It is not uncommon to hear someone saying their father was not there for them when they needed them the most. Fathers may have competing priorities, which can diminish the support the son requires. I am not supporting or giving excuses for absent fathers—every father's main priority should be their family. It can be a challenge in large families, but children will notice the father's effort and cut him some slack. If the whole general support aspect gets bound by love and respect, everything else gets accepted as it comes. Material abundance should not be a substitute for an abundance of love.

2. Communication

I know I can say something to you while my body says the opposite, which can be anyone's guilt. We feel it when we receive or pass mixed messages. Thanks for mentioning communication, Son. Many distractions can affect relationships; mobile phones, TVs, and working from home are some of the diversions that can take my full attention from some conversations. I am guilty of giving divided attention at some stages, yes. As parents, we get immersed in our work world or whatever occupies our minds and neglect the most important parenting duty, communicating well with our kids. All device interactions should momentarily cease when we have conversations that require our full attention. Do you have an incident you would like us to discuss, Son? Do you feel we are missing the mark?

Sure, Dad. Sometimes you prejudge before you hear my side of the story and are too repetitive with what you say, Junior answered.

I'm very much guilty of that, for sure. I have told you before that I would like to change some of the styles passed down by past generations. Our communication styles follow our progression as we evolve, but some ancient aspects evade time until a circuit breaker stops its flow to the next phase.

Yearning for our kids to be better than us is common in most parents. There are exceptions, of course, where some compete with their kids, which is healthy if it is an encouragement tool accepted by both, but detrimental if it breeds disharmony. You are prone to making similar mistakes to the ones I made growing up, as my DNA is part of you; knowing my flaws will help you understand yourself and adjust accordingly. Take all the flaws that you do not like in me, accept and work on them. These flaws flow in us and need to be worked on to prevent face-planting yourself due to known issues. No topic is sacred or off-limits with me, Son, unlike my dad and the ones before him in my culture, where uncles and aunts had designated roles to educate their nephews and nieces on sexually related matters. I see why you picked communication; it could be that you notice some discomfort on my part or your part; I tell you now, Son, there is no need to feel that way. Bring the subject on, and we will discuss it until we are comfortable with any outcome. We have discussed money, budgeting, social media, peer pressure and spirituality separately. However, we can open and close these subjects, as these keep recurring in our lives until the end of our time. I know parents can overreact, be too critical, too comparative, too blaming or can even attack, ignore our responsibilities, become 'apology reluctant' and disregard feelings and needs. Yes, it is the way we were brought up that made us who we are.

3. Verbal affirmations

Sometimes I want to know how you feel about my achievements, Dad, that's why I have included verbal affirmation, Junior said.

I am right here in your corner, Son, a couple of steps back, with an ice pack, a water bottle and a towel. The fight can be fun and formidable but know that you are not alone. Dad counts the punches and will advise if you need to throw more points to win the fight. Your hard work never goes unnoticed, and I commend you for your powerful double jabs, uppercuts, or remarkable ducking. Yes, we all need someone in our corner to comfort and encourage us. I am here for you; never should you doubt my presence walking beside you. It will never be difficult for me to mention the words 'I love you, Son,' as I first said those words a few minutes after you were born, lying on my bare chest in the birthing unit in Claybank Clinic, Gweru. The bond that binds us is vital and not to be severed by any challenges we come across separately in our lives, and never should a parent lose the love for their child as the child is a product of their creation.

I have more of the words I said first to the tiny little you but have been saying them in different variations, like 'I am proud of you, Son'; you are still as special as the day you were born and you deserve all the praise a parent can give their child.

I get it, Son, why you have raised the verbally affirming point. It is essential to have positive affirmations from our parents; we want to be told when we are doing well and corrected when making errors, all in good faith. We can get a million friends and community cheering for us, but it will still feel insufficient if our parents are not on the list. Never feel inadequate. I have your back, now and forever.

However, do not feel the need to seek validation from the outside world, as that can affect your self-esteem negatively, if you are not getting confirmation in the exact form you want and when you want it. It can lead to anxiety and depression. It could be positive, if you hit the number of 'likes' you want, but it is ephemeral as it puts you in a continuous loop to satisfy the craving you created; you are the best person to give yourself any validation you need. When you are happy with your outcomes, anyone's view of the world is secondary; acknowledge it if it comes your way, but never stress if it does not. Yes, I will be there by your side. Also, know that a delay in the validation from your dad does not mean disacknowledgment. Nudge me, if need be, and I will always give you sincere feedback.

4. Time Together

I feel like we are no longer doing any activities now compared to before, that is why I have included the time together part, Dad, Junior said.

What can I do better, Son, from now on, or what can we do better to have the time together? Sometimes time passes by unconsciously and we realise when it's too late and can't roll back the time, I said.

I have time for my friends most of the time but I do realise that I need to spend time with you like we did when I was younger, Junior said.

We live hectic lifestyles, Son, compounded by social media and other distractions that can leave limited time to share and spend together. Knowing how and when to adjust, alter or completely transform our lifestyle can free up the necessary time. I must admit there were times that my life revolved around work or study, which left little time for us to share; no matter how I tried to make it quality time, it remained inadequate. Texting, calling or Facetime does not create the same togetherness, I responded.

I'm now twenty, Dad, and need you more than before. There is no better time than *now* as the past is gone. We are living in the now and appreciate our time together now, Junior added.

The bond can break down if there is no together-time between father and son. I don't want to make excuses and recall the past, but even though I was super busy, we had a great time-together moment. Renovating our house together was a super special, treasured moment that we will discuss for years. We enjoyed the work and the outcome without contentious issues arising, only father-son bonding. In the past, we have played soccer together, gone to school camps, to the movies, had dinners, etcetera, too. We can still do those things if we want to. We'll never be too old to be young again. A trip to several countries would be an excellent time-together moment. However, a trip around the world is a dream for many. A great time together does not have to be complicated or expensive. Such things as cutting grass together in the backyard, barbequing together, rearranging furniture, vacuuming the house, shopping, going to the barbershop, watching a match, or even watching the sunrise or sunset together—but *not seeing them as chores*—are great ways of making memories and are simple to accomplish as father and son. Is this the discussion you had in mind when you wrote your list, Son? I asked.

Yes, Dad, you have pretty much highlighted the importance of 'time together', Junior answered. All we want as children is time with our dads and to let them be our heroes; we look up to them.

I nodded in understanding, and replied, You can lose focus if a part of what makes you whole is missing in your life. Being able to look to your father is a bit like a mirror that helps you form and adjust your self-image. If the mirror is not there when you need it, you are limited in your ability to correct how you look before you walk out into the world. Without that mirror, you may begin not to care about your appearance, your confidence will drop, and this will be noticeable to the people you encounter.

5. Personal life experience advice

What we live for, how we live, and the motivation to live is inborn and for us to identify. Without giving any thought, we look forward to the 'assigned' activity of searching for food and water. After that, personal life experiences get based on the choices we make. No two individuals will have the same experience at the end of their life's journey. However, there are commonalities that we will have based on how we create our path on received advice, principles and the personal motivation to achieve our desire. I don't have all the answers and advice for life's problems, nor are they located in a single repository in order of sequence. We all make mistakes and mess up along the way. Answers to life's challenges are everywhere, but for us to identify and apply to the correct challenge. You may want to incorporate the following as a guide:

– Create an environment that will give you satisfaction and happiness without being self-centred. Joy and happiness breed more joy and happiness. Surrounding yourself with people who understand you or try to give you the edge toward your goals. You are an average of the people you spend the most time with; therefore, place yourself in the group that will foster your growth rather than suppress it. What you presently have should give you the pleasure and drive to achieve the next step without self-criticism, which takes away your happiness. Keep focusing on your desired target, and everything else will fall into place. Persistence, determination and grit will deliver your goal.

- Opportunities come and go. Make an informed decision before grabbing what may look like an opportunity. Know the difference between a need and a want, then prioritise. Never regret a missed opportunity or keep a list of regrets, as the past can never be recouped, you can only prepare for the future.

- The unhappiest lot are those who try to impress others. Impress yourself, and what others think of you is none of your business; your business is to achieve your next goal. So, treat yourself with respect and believe in yourself, as what the world sees in you is what you feel inside. Also, please give everyone the same care; there is always a lesson to learn from every encounter.

- Heartbreaks will happen; proceed on your journey and let time be the healer. Also, relationships are a work in progress if you both share the same dream to support each other. Be kind, forgive and be faithful to one another. Remember that those who get little food will have limited growth, and what you do not feed will eventually die, be it a hobby, or an emotion—anger, hatred, resentment or love. Supply enough nourishment to your relationships for them to grow well.

- Every challenge has its solution, and challenges will come in various forms. The first solution is not to make any emotional decisions—whether you're angry or ecstatic. Instead, take a step back, take a deep breath, gather your facts and proceed. Ask yourself the question, what would a wise person do here? You will come up with a much more thoughtful response.

These are some of the lessons I learned from my mistakes, Son. The advice will come in handy along your journey, but do not punish yourself if you repeat some mistakes I made along my way. Life is a journey with a terrain that keeps changing. Assess a situation before it goes pear-shaped. Adjusting your plans is much easier than resolving an issue after it has gone out of control.

We covered all of what you listed; I hope you got the responses that will light your paths in times of need, I said.

Chapter 10

Mind Reader

The ability to understand the mental state of yourself or of people you are surrounded by is terrific. Now, I know what that is through experience and maturity. Your behaviour, personality and outlook place you with a defined group in other people's eyes. The respect and treatment you get is the average treatment of your defined group. We are like bees in a beehive, each performing pre-loaded and pre-allocated tasks for the good of the hive. This goes back to how everyone and each one of us are connected; everything that we do or say is predetermined, pre-set, and with it comes buttons for different choices; we choose the path that we want to take, yes, and within that path are growth nudges that nudge us to keep on track with our chosen course. Those nudges can propel you forwards or backwards, depending on your resilience and determination, or lack thereof.

It does not matter whether you are on a 'good' or 'bad' path; the nudges, also known as challenges, will always be waiting for you on your way. Nothing and no one is inherently good or bad, as Laurence Overmire said, everything is a spectrum of expression, and there is more than one perspective on any situation or challenge. We also assign meanings to happenings and define them as good or bad, depending on how they impact our emotions. Choose what gives you joy and happiness without harming others. As an example, dinner break at FPH was between 5:30 pm and 7:00 pm. However, the canteen's scheduled close time was 6:30 pm every day. As you know, I only take my sandwich for the day, and if I finish my sandwich, that would be it, no extra eating until I get home, only coffee. I found drinking coffee helped to control my eating habits. However, the change in diet was necessitated by running out of belt-fastening hole positions, which became a worry. With the additional shift to my day job, I had to eat something around my standard dinner time. The alternative was to eat at home after my day ended at midnight, which meant that my body's rest and recovery time would be affected by the digestion period.

I locked my plan in my mind and closed 6 pm as my ideal time for supper break. Surprisingly when I got to my shift, Mohan said, 'Maxwell, your break will be at 6 pm every day as you need to get to the canteen before they close at 6:30 pm.' How uncanny, I thought. I had spent the day contemplating the best time to have my dinner, and I hadn't revealed anything to anyone.

While walking to the canteen, I couldn't help but smile and remark, 'Yep, you know what I want when I want and how I want,' to the cosmos.

Six pm became my supper break time till I left FPH. It was strange from an everyday perspective, but from the standpoint of infinite intelligence, it was no accident that the entire scene had taken place on that day, from beginning to end. Infinite intelligence understands what you desire and only offers it to you if it helps you reach your goal. Maybe I should have asked Mohan what made him give me the 6 pm slot without verbally asking for it. But when you know how the transmutation of thought energy results in things, you do not ask as you already know what has happened and what is happening.

The energy connection that connects each of us to the source directs us to those that tune in to the same thinking wave. We quickly tune into the shared wave pattern if we step out to maintain a continuous harmony for the good of all involved.

> We define happenings as good or bad. Choose what gives you joy and happiness, without harming others.

I stood in the queue waiting to buy a fish and chips meal, four months into the job. My dietary plan had shifted to eating whatever was in the canteen to fill me up. Before this job, I had eaten as few calories as possible for a few years. I was pretty picky initially, but the food choices were minimal for the afternoon shift. Despite the fewer choices in the canteen, the food was quite yummy, albeit calorie-heavy. Thursdays were my favourite, and the meal had salmon and potatoes or fries if you wanted with a bowl of mixed veggies. I must admit this was one of the most favoured healthy meals. I would have the salmon, the bowl of veggies, and a free choice of fruit, which went on the company bill.

Mohan had mentioned not to forget to get our free fruit when we went to the canteen. The company bought fruit daily to ensure every worker was getting some form of vitamins in Covid-19 times. Brilliant idea: these guys must be looking at every way of increasing morale in the workplace, I thought. With the 'Kaizen' improvement culture (a methodology for improving processes in every part of the organisation) it was no wonder that you would notice incremental changes most of the time, be it in the canteen, the changing room or our work area. Workers got rewarded for coming up with ideas for improving their work areas or any part of the plant they felt needed changes. The change needed to be supported with views on how the current setup affected the process and how the proposed changes would improve it.

I got my food and walked to an empty table, which had a view of a pool and the neatly manicured lawns and flowers; what a view it was. Whether or not you love gardening, the picturesque views would calm you down and invite you to take a walk after your meal. But, unfortunately, break time had a limitation of thirty minutes. So, you either had to shovel your food down your gut and take a leisurely walk till break time ran out, or you had to sit, enjoy your food, and savour the views from the comfort of the canteen chair, which is what I did most of the time.

As I sat enjoying the undisturbed views and the rich salmon taste, Donne, my friend, came over and sat in the opposite vacant chair. Donne had recently moved to this country. We both came from the southern part of the motherland; we were melanin opposites. Despite the difference used as a measure by generations before to divide humanity, we both could relate to the sound of the common crow in the distance, baboons barking, wahoos, the laughing dove, the red-eyed dove and the red-necked dove singing tunes. Every time we reminisced about life back home, you could feel and touch her passion for her roots, like anyone who had migrated from that part of the world. Unfortunately, our circumstances had pushed us to re-orientate, recalibrate and ignore the motherland's pull, and fly some twelve thousand eight hundred kilometres from the nest to build a new, more comfortable one.

We tend to get pulled to cities, towns or places that are similar in some way to the environment we grew up in or spent the most time in.

However, the challenges arise when you move to a city that offers everything you aspire to but excludes the 'nest' itself due to exorbitant asking prices. Acquiring or building a nest of your own is a challenge that most who migrate do not quite understand or envision until they start the process. Overcoming the challenge can be simplified if you come with a working partner—you can jointly save and raise the required mortgage deposit faster than with a single income. Alternatively, the easier way is to relocate to a more affordable city, town or place with acceptable amenities. Suppose I was to advise anyone stepping their foot in this country for the first time with the aim of settling here. In that case, my advice would be that they should go to towns where houses are affordable, buy a place, wait a couple of years for it to appreciate, then move to their desired city. You might change your perspective entirely and remain in that affordable location. It is not the size of the town that gives you comfort but the size of the house and the reception you get at home when you step in after a day's work, with or without family.

My chats with Donne centred around settling in this new beloved country of choice. I would ensure that whatever topic we discussed over our break periods on the days we bumped into each other would always be uplifting and spirit-building, not moaning and wallowing.

In my earlier years in this country, I met some individuals who were frustrated with their lives. Before you know it, after a chat with such people, you would feel emotionally drained and as negative as them.

What is important is to protect your candlelight from being blown out by anyone, just like on Candlemas night. Growing up Catholic, our church building was a kilometre away from our house. We walked to church as we did not have a car. As young boys, we would try to protect our candlelight from being blown out by the wind or by our peers on our walk home from Candlemas. Getting home with the candlelight still flickering was a significant achievement. The effort we put into protecting the flame from being blown out by unwanted elements is the effort we should put into protecting our emotions.

When you notice the gradient of any discussion tipping your mood from happiness to sadness, change the subject or excuse yourself and move away from the conversation. The after-effects can be long-lasting and have ripple effects that creep into other parts of your life. The unfortunate thing about such people is that they could be your mates. However, it's important to notice the negativity when they emit it, and how it leaves you emotionally upset and drained.

On your part, Son, always keep a 'bag' of compliments. Hand them out at every appropriate time in your chats, regardless of who the conversation is with: a stranger, classmate, workmate, friend, boss, business associate or anyone. Your bag of compliments will have a dual effect: on you and on the person receiving the praise.

You can set out the number of compliments you want to receive per day. You will get two if you give out two; you will get four if you compliment four people per day; you will get ten compliments if you praise ten people per day, and at the end of the day, if your compliments are genuine, you will be that much more uplifted and happier. The other thing you need to know, Son, is that 'happy' and 'sad' are the same.

Draw a line and label one end happy and the other sad—the centre resembling nothing, no happiness, and no sadness. So, when you compliment someone and make them 'happy', you are pulled towards the happy end. You make another person happy; they keep drawing you towards the pleased end. The converse also has the same impact regardless of how far from the centre you are when you make someone unhappy irrespective of the circumstance. There is no justification for making anyone miserable. You might not feel sad, but nothing close to happy—something worth noting. If you intentionally make someone depressed, you get pulled to the 'sad' end. You hurt someone, and you get drawn to the 'sad' end. If you keep on with that behaviour, you remain on the sad half of the line. But you might say, what about sadists who enjoy another person's pain? But studies like that of David Chester and others in the *Personality and Social Psychology Bulletin* on 'Sadism and Aggressive Behaviour' (2018) show that sadistic behaviour ultimately deprives the sadist of happiness.

We are placed on this planet to enjoy life and be happy. We only get the opposite if we ignore our inborn wants.

What we desire and want for ourselves emotionally is the same as the next person's wants and desires. These are the basic principles for being human and being here. So, if you deprive others of what you have, through your selfishness, greed or hatred, know that whatever you have denied through actions or inaction will be taken away from you one way or the other. Such is the game of life.

The rules are simple, but we choose to ignore them like a driver going through a red light because no one is watching him. If we keep to the rules, they keep us, and if we break them, they will hurt us.

The authorities have the same effect as the law of gravity, and you are born attached to them. You cannot hide and break the rules and think no one has seen you in the act. See, if you disregard the law of gravity, you fall from a tree, a cliff, the roof of your house or a stepladder, even if no one sees you. When you break the law, you drop onto the ground and your next action is stopped, which is the same effect as the gravitational law. The results are evident daily if you look at how your life progresses. If you are honest, you can link your achievements and adversities to your acts and deeds. You do not get excused for not knowing the laws since the laws are part of you.

Which reminds me of you, Son; when you were a newborn, your mum bathing you in your tiny bathtub, you would clutch and cling to the edges of your little tub for fear of falling. No one had taught you that you would get hurt if you fell. Such are the laws that govern us throughout this game of life. We come out of our mothers' wombs clutching the complete list of what we should follow until we depart, regardless of one's belief—be it Hinduism, Buddhism,

Judaism, Taoism, Zoroastrianism, Jainism, Shinto, Atheism, Bahai faith, Confucianism, Polytheism, Monotheism, Traditional African religion or Christian beliefs.

All these religions have some commonalities in them. Those common elements are variants of the universal laws that know no region, race, border, boundary, language, ethnicity, skin colour, hair texture, high IQ or lack thereof.

All religions are vital as they play a role to those in quest of enlightenment; religions are primers for those seeking answers. And those who are not self-limiting will continue pursuing the essence of their purpose on this planet.

****

It is a fact that being in this world without any guiding principles, laws, or advisors is like entering a pitch-dark house with no windows and furniture strewn all over the house. Everything you ever need for your comfort and leisure is in there, but nothing is in its proper place as there is no appropriate place for anything; you don't know what is in the house, but it is what you need.

Your exit is different from your entrance. You have no choice but to organise your space in that house from the moment you enter it; you get tripped, fall, pick yourself up and move whatever has tripped you out of the way. How you remove and place that item determines your ease of movement. If you throw the thing ahead of you, you will get tripped and fall again, perhaps with serious injury. Some injuries will be minor, and some will take longer to recuperate from. It will be of great importance to remember how you move. Having a solid feel for the item while moving it into a pitch-dark house is critical. As you work to make your home habitable, you will find similar problems in different rooms. You will become more comfortable in your home as you overcome these obstacles. Only the past furniture configurations in that section of the hallway will be visible to you; you will not see what is lying ahead. You can step back into the light to view your arrangement, and you will have the option of changing and rearranging the furniture if you do not like your initial setup. Some furniture will be quick and easy to arrange, and some will require more effort. As you move from the hallway to the kitchen, the situation will remain the same; despite getting accustomed to the pitch-black house, your vision will not improve. Only your mind's view will guide you through, as you will be able to envision what lies ahead.

Your reward will come as lighting that shines where you have cleared, arranged and rearranged the furniture; it will also come as inner satisfaction from your accomplishments. You will get the pleasure of walking from the entrance hallway to the kitchen, back and forth as you please—remembering the past.

Your past success will give you the urge to move to the next challenge, and you will not be able to tell what lies ahead; there will be doors in the kitchen that lead to your next challenge. All these challenges will be time-bound. The longer you take clearing one spot, the shorter time you will have to enjoy a whole cleared house.

If you are too slow, your time could end after clearing the hallway and the kitchen. Also, any of the kitchen doors could be the exit door. Like the entrance door, when you exit, there is no option of returning to the house unless a divine intervention is possible. If you choose internal doors, the passage will lead into the lounge, toilet or bathroom, and the clearing process will continue, the contents of the house being revealed after you complete each task.

However, all these can be half tasks if you have guiding principles, laws you abide by, or an advisor who can recommend instructions from their own dark house. Each one of us is met by our advisors when we make the grand entrance into this world.

The advisor's task is to nurture and advise us of what lies ahead, either as a way of supporting or correcting our habits.

All this is tricky because you have free will, which you use more as you mature and make your own decisions. Simultaneously, the advisor is in his own dark house with no windows and is busy moving and clearing furniture out of his own way. He cannot leave his home and come into your house to help you clear your way. He can only tell you which way to go from his house, and you can choose to follow what he says or not. He knows where doors lead when you clear the kitchen, as he has been through that task before.

He knows which door opens the lounge, which opens the bathroom, the bedroom, the study and the balcony. To him, the doors have numbers as you communicate with him. You can tell him that you want the door leading to the bathroom, and he will say open the first door to your left or give instructions on how to number the doors. Then he will provide you with the door number to open. It will be up to you to follow what he says, as whatever door you choose to open, you cannot close. Neither can you open two doors simultaneously; the arranging and clearing of the room you have opened needs to be completed before opening another door. You have yourself to blame if you do not follow your advisor's advice.

There are two sides to everything that you encounter in this universe. There are always options, everything has a dual effect and you can analyse and select which one works for you. Your advisor has your best interests at heart. He completes his assigned task by providing the correct version of what he failed to do in his duties. If your advisor provides misleading information, you can go through the same mistakes, but he will suffer the consequences of his misleading information more than you.

That reminds me of a sad incident I encountered the other year at my rental property. The property was vacant due to renovations. So, a few days after Christmas, I went to check everything was okay, cut the lawns and clear the mail from the letterbox as the house insurance policy advised. Most of the letters were junk mail, but one letter caught my attention. It was in a brown envelope with a Department of Corrections stamp and partially opened.

The name on the letter was not someone who had rented my property as far as I knew. The partially opened letter raised my curiosity. I threw the junk letters in the recycling bin and proceeded into the house with the letter. I thought of ringing my former property manager to ask if she would know this person. Still, with Christmas break, she would not be back to work for another week; I did not want to bother her, so I cancelled that option. I looked at the letter and wondered if forwarding information could be in the contents of the letter. I was looking for justification for opening it. Finally, I said to myself, 'Open it, Maxwell, the writer could be needing assistance—it's Christmas time.'

I carefully opened the letter and went on to read it. The person was a son writing to his mum. He was in prison and was to be released a week before Christmas and wanted someone to pick him up from jail. He regretted going off the rails and wanted a clean slate for his son. Unfortunately, he could not reach out to his ex-partner as she was living with another man. The letter went on to say that his dad could not pick him up either as he had been arrested a few days after himself for a different case. The dad had been living in another city, but when he got arrested, he was imprisoned in the same jail as his son—a poignant letter.

The son had come into this world and been welcomed by his advisor, his dad, who was still busy trying to find his way into the kitchen in his own darkened house. If the advisor has not progressed into the next room, it becomes impossible for the advisee to receive the correct information to progress and open the next door. As everything is time-bound, time would probably run out before the advisor and the advisee can clear and enjoy the lounge or the bedroom. And the cycle will carry on to the son's son until one of the two breaks the pattern, which still takes twice the effort. However, the grandson will move quicker than the father if the father fulfils his advisor role.

As you grow up, your 'free will' guides you to all the options you can ever have from the trustworthy advisors you need. The purpose is to learn, grow, and use what you came out holding as your guiding principles. Your intuition will always come to your assistance if you need to change or break away from a corrosive upbringing. If you have the passion, you will break the cycle.

I went to school with some kids whose fathers were known for the wrong reasons in our community; if anybody wanted to give an example of bad parenting, the name of the father of Jabu, one of my classmates, would always come up. The father abused alcohol and his treatment of his kids was the 'how not to treat your kids' example. What also worsened the plight of my classmate was that the dad was a single dad, and there was no social system to assist kids in such predicaments as Jabu.

Education was cramming and regurgitating a lot of useless information; thank God we have Google now. I remember questions like 'How many legs does a locust have?', 'What is the longest river found on each continent?', 'Who was Shaka's mother?', 'What was Mfecane?' and so on. Jabu did not have the gift of memory retention, but he had determination. Jabu knew his limitations, so he concentrated on the subjects he knew would help him escape his upbringing. Jabu did not let his dad's alcoholism destroy what he set out to achieve.

Jabu and his three siblings lived in a one-bedroom semi-detached house. Studying or doing homework, for Jabu, was impossible. Disturbances would come from his dad, who came home inebriated most of the time, with no kind words for him. Jabu's mum had separated from his father. Sometimes Jabu's dad would take his anger out on the kids, upsetting Jabu's studying progress.

The neighbours did not make his studying easier, either. In the semi-detached house they lived in, the walls were 'paper-thin' so that any sound from the neighbours who got home, equally inebriated, was amplified. In addition, the neighbour brought home a different woman every night.

The houses were so close that you could hear the neighbour's sneezing or his stomach rumbling. There was nothing discreet about these homes, to the point where Jabu liked narrating some of the stories he would overhear from the neighbour's many women friends. There was no community library that Jabu could go to other than the school's library, which closed at 5 pm. However, school classrooms were left open for anyone who wanted to continue studying until 10 pm, which Jabu used to reach his goal. He spent most of his time in the school classrooms after regular classes, studying or discussing with equally motivated students. It was apparent to us from watching our peers graduate that you either had to pass your subjects or you would end up not much different from your parents.

A lesson I learned from one of my high school teachers was that his students' 'success' was to exceed what their parents had achieved, academically and financially. I'm not sure if his philosophy applies to Bill Gates, Jeff Bezos, or Elon Musk's kids now; the philosophy was relative. He would have probably used a different motivational talk in another school decile. Nevertheless, the teacher motivated Jabu, me and the rest who took his advice to achieve better than our parents. For Jabu, it was much more than school achievement. He was determined to remove his siblings from the toxic environment they were in. It was about grasping opportunities and running with them until he reached success.

Jabu excelled in his chosen subjects and went on to university.

He chose a well-rewarded profession and then changed the course of his siblings' otherwise ill-fated lives. He moved from the passage in that dark house into the kitchen and went past where his dad was stuck. With the help of other advisors, and his intuition, he progressed.

The wheel rotates where the will is and takes you to the destination you desire. Jabu overcame only one part of his assignment on this planet; he is still in his pitch-dark house, and so is his dad. Busy groping, moving and clearing the path so they can both move and enjoy the vacated space with light in it.

Remember how the furniture feels in the dark, should you come across it again, and how best to move without causing harm to yourself or your advisee. Giving bad advice to your advisee will cause you not to progress and enjoy the next space or room in your own house.

A couple of months ago, my dad was a bit upset because I had not rung him for over a month. He sent me a sour message through WhatsApp, voicing his frustration. He had a good point, which I acknowledged. However, you, Son, when you go to your mum's house, usually ring me every second day to check on me and update me on how your lectures are going, and when you don't call, I get worried. On this week, you had not rung. You can imagine how I was feeling, and simultaneously my dad was sending me a message that I had not called or messaged him in a month. The way I was feeling for you not ringing was only a quarter of what my dad felt anticipating my call.

The following day I rang my dad through WhatsApp, which did not go through because of a poor network. I made two more attempts and was not successful. I gave up and sent him a recorded message to say that I had tried to call him and the network on his side was a bit 'drunk', so I could not connect. As soon as I pressed the send button for the message to my dad, you rang me from your mum's place. I went, *wow!* when I saw your name as the person ringing. And then, when I answered, you went on to give a lame excuse for not ringing me, and I said yep, Son, I know why. I knew I had not rung my dad, and it was a reverse effect coming from the other side and feeling the impact of not calling one's dad.

I am in my own dark house just like anyone else; you are in your dark house, too. I have managed to clear piled-up furniture out of my way, and there is light from the entrance up to where I am now. As for you, I am giving you all that I know, which will help you clear your way and have light where you are moving. The experiences and knowledge I have gained over the years I have been on this planet will help you move forward. My sincere intentions and hope are that all the information I give you is worth having and adds to your knowledge bank, which you will withdraw one day should you need it to clear a hurdle on your way forward. I am getting on in life but do not have all the information and advice you might need. I am learning as I move around my dark house. You are teaching me as you move forward in your dark house. Our roles are interchangeable and complimentary, albeit I have a broader role than yours.

When you fail to clear and organise furniture out of your way, I have equally failed. When one of us fails, both of us have flunked, making it crucial that apart from being father and son, you and I are conjoined as we progress in life. It is like an educational system that evaluates teachers based on their pupils' exam scores. I, as your parent, rank myself according to how you are progressing in life. There is no exam, but continual assessments require me to advise you continuously, and the universe scores me on your performance.

Like the assessments I was getting from Mohan and Rod at FPH—I looked forward to the evaluations as they were always some takeaways after the meetings. The assessments were once every three months, and with open discussion, you were allowed to express how you felt you were progressing in the assigned tasks. If you thought the training was inadequate, you had the opportunity to air that out, and if you thought you were getting unfair treatment, you would say it. My position would have been different from someone who had this job as their only job. Studies have shown that lower-level employees are not as open and free with giving out workplace feedback when asked on a one-on-one level. Knowing that I was there to learn from all the activities and procedures gave me a sense of self-assurance. As much as Rod and Mohan made me feel comfortable before the start of the appraisal, I probably made them feel at ease, too, more so during our first session.

My primary job had a biannual process, so I let them know that I had undergone this process before, so it was familiar. What was not familiar was how they were to structure the process.

Training was embedded in all the processes at FPH. Every section department had a trainer as part of the team. After completing any activity, you would sign that you have undertaken the training, and the signed document would go in your file, which is the file Rod would bring along on the assessment day. Mohan had my training plan with him and all the assessments I had done, and he notified me of all upcoming training scheduled ahead of time. Statements like, 'Keep doing what you are doing', 'Your team is here to help you', 'Is there anything you want us to do to help you with?' and 'Don't hesitate to ask if something is unclear' were always part of the conversation.

Performance appraisals are about touching base with your subordinate and finding ways to improve them and yourself as their leader; It is a two-way process, not to be approached with dread by associates. They will notice if you are genuinely interested in improving them or if you only want to complete the process required by your job description. Some organisations tie this process to a reward system, which my primary employer has.

I had one bad experience a few years back. I still have the evidence as an example to show how the system was being manipulated, abused and corrupted to benefit a few who fell into a particular group in the organisation. When the time came for the year's final assessment, my manager notified me a few days before the date. We set an appropriate time best suited to our calendar availability. We had set goals for the year and periodically checked in to review the progress. On the final assessment for the year, the process involved rating myself and then my manager rating me based on how well we achieved the goals, on a scale from one to five, with five being the highest possible ranking.

Based on the goals set, I had done well. My manager ranked me to reflect my achievement, and I was happy with how he had ranked me. Ronald, my immediate boss, handed the completed forms to our department manager, Pete, who signed the documents and agreed with the performance rankings. He signed his part and gave the papers to his boss, who was well above me in the organisational structure; there were two managers above me, and he was third in the line of command. This manager told Pete and Ronald that I was not good enough to get those high rankings, scribbled on the forms, sent them back through the same chain, and then went on to tell Ronald to rank me as ones and twos. Ronald said to him that I was his direct report. He knew my performance; how he had rated me was how he had monitored my performance over the year. Giving me lower marks, ones and twos, did not sit well with his conscience. He refused to take recommendations that came from a boss who did not know my daily performance and with no direct reporting. A new form was filled in with no changes and handed back. He sat on the completed appraisal forms refusing to hand them over to HR. And that is how my review for that year ended—with nowhere to appeal.

I got the minimum increment, no other incentive, and no bonus. Everyone else in the department got hefty bonuses, and the department had more cash to share as one was left off the list: me. Performance did not matter; what mattered was being part of a 'group'. No one had the power to change that setup; even though my colleagues saw the injustice, they were powerless. I do not have resentment, but I have kept the documents for reference whenever I reflect on my years in that organisation.

Unpleasant incidents can put your emotions into a tailspin and may rekindle and inflame the simmering pain within you if you do not get closure. However, I have learned to take these incidents, pleasant or unpleasant, as life's lessons. Every adversity is a process of purification. I always ask myself, 'What was the universe teaching me then?' or 'What am I learning from what is unfolding in front of me?'

Do not lose hope when you try and fail to get what you feel you deserve. It was probably not yours at that point, but you will get it when the time is right, two, three, four or fivefold. What belongs to you in this life, you do not lose. Remember, we are here to enjoy and win this game of life. Whoever is standing between you and your desires will falter and fall. The duration of the time they spent blocking your way is the time set aside and required for you to grow out of that current self and prepare for better treasures. You will eventually walk over that person to claim your glory on the podium like Valerie Adams over Nadzeya Opstachuk in the 2012 Olympics when the latter failed a drug test in the shotput event. You must note that your effort might also be rewarded in other forms. The obstacles become part of the way.

The universe has many ways and forms of compensating you for what is rightfully yours. Looking around, you will notice all the blessings that have come walking into your life to give you the joy you thought had passed you. A son, a daughter, a partner, or a business could have been among your many blessings. They may have also arrived in the form of your house, bed, timepiece, companion, health or even your supply of energy. Everything you have in life is a reward you've earned.

Remember that someone else yearns for what you have, but they're still waiting in queue for their turn. If you feel and think life is giving you a raw deal, you end up getting that raw deal if you spend your mental energy connecting to those raw deal thoughts. The satisfaction you get from anything starts with your thoughts and transmutes into your being. A victim mentality leads you nowhere but only awards you its fruit: perpetual dissatisfaction, misery and resentment.

We all know someone who is always in that state of gloominess, miserableness, mope and low spirits. The perpetual dissatisfaction becomes part of their self. No one is born with discontent in their DNA.

There is positive dissatisfaction and negative dissatisfaction that rule our lives. We are where we are as the human species because of positive dissatisfaction. Every improvement and development happened because someone was dissatisfied with the status quo, which led them to seek better ways to improve the scenario. So we go to school, pursue education, jobs, better jobs, build houses, better houses; we invented cars, and then found ways to improve the cars' emissions; we invented mobile phones. It's all positive dissatisfaction with inbuilt excitement. The excitement of achieving a result that transforms the things we don't like.

All of us who go to work, regardless of the location, work because of dissatisfaction, within us, within our country, within the planet. We want to improve what we can. When we have improved what we sought to improve, we get dissatisfied again, so we look for something else to fix. The cycle will continue until we pass on to the next dimension, leaving the planet improved.

Negative dissatisfaction has inbuilt gloominess. Instead of improving the unsatisfactory status quo, the person will be stuck or make no effort to change their circumstance. These people drain your energy with negativity, whining, moaning and grumbling. When you start finding faults in anything and everything and these thoughts are accompanied by anger and hatred, know that the time is ripe to rewind, replay, edit and cut off the parts that are of no benefit to yourself, your family, your friends and society at large. Cut out the fussing, bleating and fuming out of your act. Otherwise, you will end up with a health condition born out of your unhappiness.

My performance appraisal at FPH went as well as expected and anticipated, with the words 'Keep doing what you are doing' coming from Rod, the Stores Manager. I had shown no interest in applying for any permanent role as I had been urged to do by Mohan, my supervisor, but I kept performing like someone keen to get a permanent position. One should not limit or excel in job performance based on job security. A performer is always a performer, whether in a one-day role or a permanent role. Being your best is always good for you as you may fall back on that performance one day.

A day after the appraisal, Mohan told me I was to go and work in another building, servicing the needs of that production area on my own. He would give me a phone should I get stuck. I would give him a call, and he would assist. Being trustworthy is very important in whoever you deal with, whether it's a spouse, girlfriend, friend or family member. What matters is that you must fulfil what you promised to the best of your ability. It is easy to notice if someone short-changes you in personal relationships or work situations. When it comes to getting a position of responsibility, your performance will come to your assistance if the organisation and its systems are fair and continuously audited to identify, remove, and correct biases that might creep in.

Most work systems get designed with good intentions. For example, a good HR department will go out of its way annually to teach, explain and update its company's policies, vision and benefits to employees, and not only come out when there is employee disciplining or a grievance. Some HR departments are good with candidates during recruitment and selection, but, once the employee has joined the organisation, the relationship weakens.

Serving the needs of more than fifty production staff on my own was quite exciting as I got to meet, know and talk to a whole new set of the team. Production staff would request and pull spares through the 'Kanban' process system, an inventory management process that triggers an order when parts and materials are low. The printer would spit out the tickets from my end in the warehouse, and I would pick up the orders using a tow truck and deliver the parts to the production area. The rate of pull would vary depending on the production targets. Busy days were Mondays and things would ease up as the week progressed. Some days were relatively slow; reading a book or listening to a podcast cranked up the time.

I got to meet and listen to stories from an ethnically diverse group of people, as it is the culture of FPH recruitment policy to be inclusive. One such person was Leila, the supervisor of the whole production floor. At the end of each shift, with the help of her team leaders, she would stand at the production floor's exit door and thank her staff for a good shift. It was more like what the netballers do at the end of their matches.

I became curious the first time I saw everyone in a single file, Leila at the door talking to everyone going past her. So, after everyone had left, I went to ask her what the single file was about, and she said, 'Oh, it's how I thank my staff. Some of them are young and it's their first time on a job.' Most of them were girls and young women who played some form of sport, and bringing that sportsmanship to the work environment was what every team member understood. Everyone was part of the team, and everyone was valued. Leila, the team coach, was grateful to have them in her group, and so that was her message at the end of the shift.

What a strategy, I thought to myself. Being a good motivator requires identifying what is relatable to everyone and using it as a basis and foundation for anything you want to build on. That way, everyone will understand and feel valued each time they come to work. A bit of micromanaging is necessary for the newbies, but once they know their roles and develop confidence, the set targets get achieved most of the time. Most of the tasks performed in the production were simplified so that anyone with a primary education could follow, quickly learn, and understand them.

It was a great strategy from FPH. Production processes need simplification for any production organisation to realise and achieve its goals and targets. It should be easy to train the next person, like in the fast-food industry where anyone can run a production line if given clear and structured work instructions. Turnover can then be high, like at McDonald's, and the business can cope with it. But that high turnover also gets overcome by a good 'hygienic factors' culture that values, respects and develops its workforce, and offers competitive wages or salaries.

A week before I transferred to Leila's building, my department had celebrated Tina's thirty-five-years-long service award, which is an outstanding achievement by any standard. To have someone work for a single company for that long, like Nixon in my primary company, means that the company meets the employee's needs and is thus commendable.

****

Eight months into my job, I got invited to the 'main' stores where Mohan and his crew were based so we could watch the end-of-financial-year presentation on the stores' monitor as a team. Rod was there too. The event had happened during the day. However, it got recorded for those who missed the live speech so that we could watch it when we turned up for our shift. Everyone was looking forward to the announcement.

The results for the first half of the year got reported just after I joined the company in March for the previous year, and everyone who had worked for the company in the last year had received a bonus. The bonus was for full-time employees only. I was interested to know how the company had performed in the past six months during the Covid-19 pandemic, the profit and projected growth—that sort of news. A week before this presentation, the company had a press release that they were revising the projected figures as demand for their products had increased considerably, which is always welcome news for any investor.

Employees had been receiving production bonuses with every financial report. However, with this one, they were expecting more than they had received in previous years based on how the company had performed on production targets and customer demand.

The screen monitor was by the open office. Open offices are one setup I observed in my primary organisation's head offices in the US, when I went there for training. Still, it had not cascaded to all regional plants because of the setup of existing buildings. Despite that, renovations could transform the buildings into open offices. For example, here at FPH, there were no doors to go into the CEO's or GM's office. Their workspaces and desks were 'open' and 'accessible'. I had heard organisations saying they have an 'open-door policy' when what they mean is the CEO or managers are behind the walls, but the doors are open. If there was a comparison, FPH was miles ahead with the 'open-door policy' strategy.

We made a horseshoe assembly, looking at the monitor as the CEO talked about how the company had done well and how it had broken all production and financial records. It was music to everyone's ears as, first and foremost, as an employee of any organisation, you want to know how safe your job is before salary increments and bonuses. After the CEO had finished, he handed over to the HR person he was co-presenting with.

It must have been her first big presentation as you could notice her uneasiness. Finally, she announced that the company would give every employee and contractor employed since July sixty-four hours of their hourly rate as bonus pay on the next payday. It was on a Tuesday, and the next payday was Wednesday. I was the first to clap my hands, and everyone followed suit. It was impressive. I was impressed by the whole announcement process. After the presentation, Rod went on to congratulate and thank everyone. It was a first for the company to award its contractors a bonus. The bonus would be the same as the one for permanent employees; the HR lady said everyone's contribution was valued, whether they were cleaning toilets, cooking in the canteen or managing a team. Impressive and inclusive indeed.

I had missed out on bonuses in my primary company despite achieving set targets because of a skewed incentive programme open to abuse. The strength you can grow from missing out is incredible, that is, if you believe in yourself. It is important to remember that you always have an opportunity waiting for you to use somewhere out there. Looking more in areas you have not searched for before would be best. With a surplus, a little effort and sacrifice can reap rewards that cover what you have missed.

I remember taking a day off back then to go and open an investment account with Forsyth Barr investment firm when I missed a bonus at my primary job. I played around with the investment demo apps on my phone to get an idea of what I was getting myself into, familiarising myself with the feeling of making gains and losses. The most brilliant way for me was to use an investment firm initially, then, as I gained confidence and knowledge, to do it alone with minimum assistance.

I rang up several investment firms to find out about their services and fees a week before and then settled on Forsyth Barr as their services were more attractive than the rest. I felt like I had already achieved my dreams as I walked through the revolving doors and was guided to the thirteenth floor of the imposing Shortland Street building in Auckland. After reaching the thirteenth floor, I walked to the receptionist, who greeted me with a professional, friendly smile and advised me to wait by the couches and my investment advisor would come and take me to his office.

The views overlooking the Hauraki Gulf were stunning, the blue waters encased by greenery from Saint Heliers to the south, Devonport to the North and Rangitoto to the East.

Views like these are therapeutic, I thought to myself. The urge to take a couple of selfies overtook me. As I took the fifth shot, Dan S, my new investment advisor, walked towards me smiling and said, 'What a beautiful sunny day.'

'Indeed,' I said, then verbalising my thoughts: 'All one needs to do is sit on these relaxing couches, savour nature's beauty, and all stress will melt away.'

'It is a beautiful view,' he said as he stretched out his hand for a handshake. 'You must be Maxwell M-koki,' he said as he struggled to pronounce my surname.

Yes, 'Maxwell MuhCoky,' I clarified, shaking his hand.

He laughed and said, 'Easy, I can say that.' Then he said, 'Dan S is my name. I will be looking after your investment matters,' as he led me to his office.

Unfortunately, the office had no views, and the purpose was probably to remove the client's distraction when giving out crucial investment advice. I did not comment about the office. My brain was racing and preparing to soak in all the investment advice I was about to be served.

I filled in the forms, which required a photocopy of my identity document. Dan asked me a range of questions, like my age, financial targets, capital and preference for stocks, and then he tailored his advice based on my answers. He only gave out advice, information, and updates. The final decision rests upon the investor, which is how I ended up with FPH in my portfolio. I got all the bonuses I missed out on at work through dividends. The first couple of stock dividends came as cheques in the letterbox. I remember my heart racing, hands shaking with an ear-to-ear grin covering my face—a delightful experience.

Dan's advice was that as it was close to reporting season, I would get dividends immediately if I bought the securities on his list.

After receiving my first dividend cheque, I gave Dan a call the following day and thanked him. Have you ever noticed that there are people you sync with at first glance, and the level of understanding of each other will be far greater than average, and so is the trust at that moment? It was Dan's job, and the training would have prepared him well to capture the client's trust, and yes, he caught my trust so well that I recommended him to my friends.

Most of us have the hunger and quest to develop and be developed. It gives humans the purpose of living and looking forward to the next day, week, month or year. We consciously or subconsciously set and give ourselves targets and goals in our lives, and tie them to some specific tasks we control, though we sometimes leave the management of our targeted outcomes to someone else. We relinquish control and hope, knowingly or not, that someone will deliver our targets to us.

Goals and targets that you set for another person, be it your son, daughter, partner, relative or even society lead to frustration, anger and resentment if that person doesn't meet them. All relationships are great before partners start setting goals for each other. First, people ensnare or attract each other into relationships. Then goal-setting kicks in, starting with setting some expectations, which progresses to asking for small favours, which will turn into mild demands and, before you know it, into commands. And when these do not get fulfilled, frustration, anger and resentment creep in, disrupting our being. And slowly, the level of love and respect falls away, and doubt enters the fray.

The same happens with relationships with our children. Parents set goals and targets for their children; these might be expectations of certain behaviours or academic goals. Likewise, children will set up expectations for their parents. When those expectations fall short, relationships get sour and strained.

If you must ask for something, ask without many expectations. Your life will flow without restriction if you lower your expectations. There will always be positive outcomes if you take that philosophy: you celebrate if you get the desired result; if not, you recalibrate. As we get frustrated in one area, we will learn from our mistakes and correct our errors. If not, someone else will be learning from our mistakes. We become examples of what to do and not to do for someone else. Such is life. Every error that you make is a valuable lesson for humanity.

Remember the day I came home from work, you were lying on your bed, and I asked out of nowhere what your purpose was in life? What a loaded question. But the truth is, it was not a loaded question; I was asking if you had ever given thought to such questions. Unfortunately, we don't give much thought or time to these questions as we cruise through this plane of life. You went to

Catholic primary, intermediate and high schools. You learnt that we need to be good people to go to heaven. Yes, excellent education indeed, but not specific.

Your answer was 'to be a good person and have a good life.' Great answer. As you work towards having a good life, you fulfil your primary purpose of being used as an example by other people and using other people's models of successes and failures to get you to the 'good life' you want. As you get to have a good life, you will notice that you will develop another desire. You might have lots of money in your bank account, excesses from your 'good life'. Then another purpose will emerge for you.

Andrew Carnegie was one of the wealthiest men of his time. He built his wealth from nothing and achieved the good life you are aiming for, and then he gave most of his money away before he died. He developed a goal that was probably his purpose in life—the ability to grow cash and then give it away to help new generations start at a better level than he did. Bill Gates, Warren Buffet, Melinda Gates, Chuck Feeney and many more have acquired enough wealth for themselves and their families. Now they are giving the excesses away to a cause, which may be fulfilling their purpose in life. Wealth, just like knowledge, is supposed to be used and shared, or else it ceases its value for you when you pass on.

I got an email from HR notifying everyone that two of our former workmates had passed on. They had all retired in the last five years; one had taken early retirement, and the other had retired at sixty-five. One wonders whether retirement takes away our purpose on this planet or whether we retire knowing that our time is about to expire and we should take time to reflect and prepare for the exit.

Nixon, my workmate who will be seventy-three this year and still working, commented on the news, adding that he has no plans to retire yet; as he said, those retiring are not lasting for long before they pass. Nixon says he does not have a hobby that will occupy his free time should he retire, other than travelling.

See, people who retired to travel and see the world got affected by Covid-19 and the closure of international travel. The idleness and inactivity can give the body the signal that it is not required much for daily routine and action, which can lead to its natural process of disintegrating and atrophy.

We have these bodies to achieve our targets, dreams and desires through movement. Thoughts and spoken words have the same effect when we converse with ourselves. So, when we tell ourselves that we no longer want to work, new options will arise that we can choose from to move our bodies. And still, when we show no interest in any options, our bodies can then get redirected to serve a new purpose. First, feeding the worms in the ground by returning to our original matter state, as the soul moves to the next plane, depending on how well it has performed its tasks.

Chapter 11

Post Announcement Mood

I witnessed two internal financial announcements as an employee for FPH, and after every announcement, all you would see on people's faces were wide grins—it was a happy workforce. Who would not be satisfied after getting a lump sum paid into their accounts? We often celebrated with a shared lunch. The joy that came after the announcements was incredible. After watching the end-of-year presentation, I returned to my workstation and was impressed not by the bonus but by the whole process, which is the stuff you find in management textbooks. It was theory in practice. I learned some years back that some practitioners do not follow management textbook material. The difference was that more than fifty university graduate trainees were recruited yearly here. When you have graduate trainees, as much as you challenge them, they also challenge and question the processes you follow, which creates a continuous learning experience for both the organisation and the graduates.

Jessica was one of the graduates I used to converse with when we bumped into each other in the canteen. She joined the organisation after researching its values, vision and fundamental principles. She felt that for her to grow and develop the skills and knowledge she'd acquired at university, this was the best place to be practising. We had the same objective but a different approach. She was practising her craft, and I was absorbing the products of her practice. I was here to experience a different work setting, and it was no disappointment.

Was it different? Was I comparing apples to apples? Was what I was comparing to in the same setting as the 'bad' experiences I had gone through? Sometimes we get lost in our quest to right what was wrong, while it has since evolved to the same level that we hold in high esteem. We fail to appreciate the total brightness of the light because of the speck of soot on our lens. Then we take the view from behind the lens with soot and assign a bright value to it. We stick to and use that imagined value to identify the brightness of the light.

The brightness of the lights is possibly the same, varying only in our perception of it. The lens alone cannot provide a figure or value that you can say, 'Yes! This light is brighter than the other.'

Three years before the Covid-19 pandemic, my primary organisation had a development programme at its head office in Ohio, Pennsylvania. I missed out for the first two years, but I kept showing interest in attending the programme. My boss then, who has since retired, said I could participate in his place as he had no interest in the training. Unfortunately, it did not happen that year as someone had put their foot ahead of me.

At times all you need to do is ask. Ask if you think an explanation is lacking, ask if you are not sure of what is happening, ask if nothing is clear, ask if you do not know where you are going, ask her out, ask him out. Ask why you are late, ask why you are not reaching your targets, ask why the promise is still pending. Ask why you are behaving differently; ask why you have doubts. Follow the 'why' question with another 'why?' If the answer is still as clear as mud, keep asking why until filtration is complete and the final solution is crystal clear. When you start asking hard questions, many things can happen between you and the other person, but two outcomes will stand out. One: you will get clear answers, or two: you will get avoided for fear of your questions.

Once I asked for my turn to go on the training, everything fell into place: flights, accommodation and transport. I had locked head office training in my development plan for the year, and my boss had to support me in achieving that goal. The support had come based on questions and discussions we'd had the previous year. No one wants to be seen as the person who stalls an organisation's strategy, more so in workplaces if there is accountability, values and vision. As a result, there was remarkable progress, gradually, in my organisation. When I joined the organisation, it transitioned into part of a multinational organisation, which had shared values and ideas.

Supporting what the organisation stood for were helpline phone numbers that employees could ring and raise issues if they felt unethical happenings were going on—this empowered staff and, at the same time, improved accountability. No one would want an email or phone call from Ohio because of a complaint against them. The acquisition and incorporation had overturned the whole Deep South experience into that of a more comprehensive 'world organisation'. Grumblings from some quarters within the local plant indicated that some were not happy with the monitoring. Those who were not satisfied were the ones with skeletons in their cupboards. Change is difficult if you are in charge and there is no external pressure to make the change. However, if you are getting a directive to change, you either must abide by the requirements or quit independently. If it pays your bills, you must grin and bear it until the resistance within yourself has evaporated or simmers without visible fissures. If it becomes noticeable, reprimand will come your way.

****

There is nothing as reassuring as being told you are valued. Whether as a child, a parent, a partner or a worker. As much as you want to be valued, know that the other person also wants to be appreciated, which goes back to being generous with your comments. Give positive comments out freely to anyone and everyone. We lose nothing but gain a light heart by giving positive comments that show how appreciative we are. We do not gain anything by being miserly with positive words. When you have something and do not use it, you are as good as someone without it. And when you have excess that someone could use and you keep it to yourself, know that eventually, you will lose control of it.

And more so with positive words, you cannot bank them for use on a rainy day. The moment you talk to someone is the right moment to say something positive. Positive comments should not be reserved and ranked according to a person's likeability. As I mentioned before, lifting your own mood is as simple as making the next person feel good about themselves, and the opposite is true. Making anyone angry or upsetting someone will never uplift your spirit. You can never have a shady tree by cutting down your neighbour's tree. Likewise, you cannot spoil someone's day because you feel miserable. Instead, it will lead to a continuing downward spiral of your bleak mood.

If you get into a position of authority, always remember to be generous with your positive reinforcement. You will feel good when you say the words and after, probably on your way home. Most people replay the day's events at leisure, which either leads to an internal smile or brews anger and resentment. Events that we tend to replay consciously or subconsciously are the events that involved emotions of anger, happiness, love or sadness, which are likely to leave emotional scars. For example, one of my former bosses told me how harshly his boss treated him when something went wrong, and I could feel his resentment towards his former boss as he narrated the stories. However, the unfortunate part was that he replicated the same harsh treatment from his former boss to his subordinates.

We are supposed to learn from every event that happens in our lives. But unfortunately, no unfortunate event happens to you for replicating your own bad treatment to another person, and such vindictiveness will not give you internal relief after you have accomplished the part. Instead, it will put you in perpetual anger so that you continue repeating the same action until you learn and recognise the root of the behaviour. That's when you can take the load off your back. Anger is like a load of bricks you carry on your shoulders every day and everywhere you go. The worst thing is that you will add another brick to your sack every time you get angry, to the point that you will no longer recognise what triggers your anger.

All you will need to do is be honest and start unloading your bindle sack brick by brick and labelling the brick with the cause. As you take the bricks out, you will get to the source of the extra weight, your anger. Remember I said that we have these events to be better people? You acknowledge the errors of your ways and set out to protect the next person, so they avoid falling into the same pitfall.

Years back, an angry storeperson at my organisation used to be peeved over nothing and everything. None of the newbies liked to go and place orders at the stores. Initially, I thought my presence was annoying as the storeman seemed agitated whenever I ordered something. After discussing my experiences with my newbie co-workers, I learned that he behaved similarly with others. The store man got suspended pending dismissal for a 'physical' altercation with a coworker a few weeks later. It had been the second complaint within two months since the newbies had started. Even though he had been doing it continuously, the pattern had grown out of hand. The storeperson was dismissed after a disciplinary hearing since his behaviour and the evidence against him were impossible to ignore. He didn't have any leg to stand on. Had he taken time to reflect and sift through his bindle sack and label his load of bricks, he could have identified the source of his anger, which he was misdirecting to anyone and everyone. Some people cheered him on, as he was bold to exhibit abhorrent behaviour toward co-workers, especially new immigrants. The unfortunate part was when he got dismissed, he was alone, with no one to cheer him on. The bricks pulled him down. Getting the bindle sack off his hands could have saved him from losing a job.

> Anger is like a load of bricks weighing you down. Take out the bricks one by one and label the cause. As you take them out, you will get to the source of the extra weight: your anger.

You need to take stock of how you are treating others. It is easy to learn and grow if you have the will. Nothing stops a person from taking a total one hundred-and-eighty-degree turn to change their behaviour. It might not be one hundred and eighty degrees, but just a few degrees toward the accepted side. It takes a consensus for a behaviour to be accepted, and as everything in the world changes, nothing stays the same forever.

You need to keep track of changes so that you don't get caught outside the changes; you can only ride them like a wave to avoid being left behind.

In life, there is always a high and a low tide, an in-breathing and an out-breathing, an advance and a retreat, a rainy season and a dry season, an El Niño and La Niña, upward and a downward like you are playing on a trampoline. Creation and distraction, birth and death. Knowing that nothing stays the same forever in any situation gives you the armour and confidence to prepare for the next pendulum swing.

The measure of the pendulum swing to the right is the measure of the pendulum swing to the left. Rhythm compensates. Low feelings can follow high emotions, and everyone has mood swings; the only difference is how others manage theirs. Blessed are those who understand their mood swings and can move to be above the swing, so that it does not affect them. Blessed are those who have also mastered the swings. The outward and inward measure does not bring any significant change to the point that they stay close to the pendulum's centre.

You might be out having fun with your friends; you should know that there will always be after-effects of the fun; by staying in control, you avoid the side effects of partying.

You might be in a relationship, and with both of you knowing there will be high and low moments, you both stay vigilant and better prepared to ride the tides together. That is if you both want to ride the wave. But unfortunately, some relationships die a natural death, while others die because of ignorance about low and high tides. The natural shifts that affect our moods. Remember, when the swing moves further away from the centre, that is, to the sunny side, it will swing back to the same extent on the dark side, unless you have mastered the art of staying on the side of the swing you want by polarising and neutralising the effects of change.

As you spend more time on this planet, you will notice and come across these swings in your life and other people's lives. The swing does not discriminate between the haves and the have-nots or choose those who become rich, poor or famous.

After going through some of the most challenging times together, with barely enough to survive but supporting each other to build a multi-million-dollar business, you will hear a couple has decided to split. After helping each other through college and university and withstanding some tough times together, after graduating and getting top jobs with fat salaries and acquiring properties together, you will hear the couple decide to quit their marriage. After migrating thousands of kilometres, settling in a foreign country, starting a new life from nothing, being there for each other. Managing to comfortably 'settle' with more wealth than they ever dreamed of in their own country, and becoming a role model couple. Next, you will hear they have decided to go their separate ways.

After discovering that they have a deep love for each other and thinking they have found their soulmates, starting a new life together, buying a house together, bringing their kids from a previous family into the newly minted family and enjoying family life together. Then, after more than ten years raising the kids together, they will decide to split.

After building a multibillion-dollar empire with charitable organisations that help the underprivileged in their own country, in third world countries, and contributing millions of dollars every year to combat polio and other preventable illnesses, playing significant roles in vaccine development and being a role model couple, next, you will hear that the couple has decided to discontinue the marriage.

After colonising almost the whole world and spreading its influence, language and culture in its colonies, consolidating its power by forming one of the most influential economic organisations in the world, next, you hear member countries pulling out, citing imbalances within. Disintegration happens.

After colonising and conquering every country on its radar, north, south, east and west, feared by every soul that hears its name across continents, changing its subjects' belief systems, and imposing its own ways of worship, disintegration happens. The Roman Empire dissolved.

After being raised by a stepfather as an illegitimate son, a boy becomes a feared king. Killing and controlling all ethnic tribes that fall within his created empire, his authority and name are synonymous with death among his subjects; he is a god of his subjects. Then the power fizzles out and disintegration happens. The Zulu kingdom breaks down.

After emerging as a hero in a war of 'liberation', a man goes on to be the most loved president in his country, promising to transform people's lives. He works towards these goals and becomes the darling of the former colonisers and his people, then the love fades, and he becomes the opposite of the reasons he liberated the country.

He thinks no one is qualified enough to be the president if he is alive and so rules with an iron fist. With time, the iron becomes rusty, and the metal knuckles lose the ability to clench the fist. And so, the disintegration process kicks in, and the president loses popularity and is forced to step down. The power has melted away and Robert Mugabe melts with it. Everything is transitory.

So, you see, Son, everything has a life of its own and when its existence ends, no remedial effort can extend or prolong its presence however much you may want it. Therefore, embracing death is as essential as embracing and celebrating a birth.

Note that there is a difference between recognising an end and giving up. In some cases, some effort may be required, and what you are facing may be a challenge and a lesson from which you can learn and improve. However, I urge you to evaluate the full facts and history of the challenge with an open mind before reaching a judgment.

Chapter 12

Soulmate

It is everyone's wish and desire to have a soulmate. I wish I could give the correct answer and advice on this matter. What I can give you, however, are some elements, characteristics, and behaviours that can help you to identify a potential partner with whom you can have a happy, long-lasting relationship. Suppose that person turns out to be your soulmate. In that case, blessed you are, for the term soulmate is quite a heavy term to use; it means that there is one individual out there you are supposed to mate with for life. Still, that individual does not come with a barcode, colour-coded name tag or telephone number that you can quickly identify, and the relationship does not always kick-start at first try and last forever. In most cases, it is trial and error until you both feel comfortable living as mates, partners, spouses or whatever term satisfies you.

Doves are one species that are blessed to find their soulmates, for when they do match, it is for eternity. There are no differences that can arise after matching. What I found interesting about doves is how the male will lead the female to prospective areas for nesting, and the female will pick the spot. The male will bring twigs to construct the nest, which is done by the female until fully completed. Male doves get exonerated for a poorly built nest—an excellent way to start a marriage, as there are no arguments and peace prevails from the start. It could be the universe's way of showing humanity the foundation to incorporate into our mating system of maintaining peace in the 'nest'. As in doves, so it can be in humans.

My advice to you, Son, is... hold on, let me prepare another cup of lemon, ginger and apple cider vinegar tea, I said, and went on as I was preparing it: My marriage with your mum reached its expiry date earlier than anticipated. Of course, no one foresaw that, but such is life. I hope yours will be a happy, long one like the doves. Try to look for kindness, loyalty and understanding in my future daughter-in-law or whomever you want to spend your life with, rather than just looks, status or excitement. Similarly, being reliable, practical, rule-following, organised and emotionally stable are important qualities.

> What to look for in a partner:
> – Kindness, loyalty and understanding (not looks, status or excitement)
> – Similarity
> – Being reliable, practical, rule-following and organised
> – Emotional stability

There is no evidence that a more extended dating period will lead to permanent marriage or that a shorter dating time will lead to early divorce. It is, however, essential to know the person you want to spend your life with before you both decide to tie the knot.

You will be studying the person during the dating period. If you dig deep enough, you will typically get an accurate portrait of the individual. Do not make the mistake of overlooking the red flags that pop up during courtship. The flags are like lights warning you what to expect should you tie the knot. Many of us are overcome by the heat of the moment until it's too 'late'. We date a person with all the things we are looking for at the forefront of our minds, only to fall deeply in love with the opposite character to the one we desired, as we have ignored all the red flags.

It is never too late to mend your love life; you can constantly adjust your requirements. It is easier to change before starting a family, as when you have kids, the kids suffer the split more than the parents. Be kind to yourself.

A kind person will always want the best out of you and build your strengths through positive encouragement. A kind person will strive to make your life easier. They will not put unnecessary demands on you to prove that you love them. They will not measure your love based on the number and value of gifts you give them but by how kind you are to them as they are to you. A kind person will share with you without any growling or complaint; A kind person will show you how to love and be loved. A kind person will show you care and compassion and share it with everyone in their life: family, friends, workmates and strangers. Their kindness will not be limited to only those they know; it will be like the air they breathe. It does not choose who inhales it. A kind person will choose their words wisely before saying anything regardless of circumstance; they know that words are not retrievable and can transform or destroy the recipient. A kind person will remind you that they are there for you and have your back. A kind person will become you, and you will become them: mates.

Finding someone who understands you is the best you can get out of any relationship. To be understood is to be loved, and understanding someone is the epitome of love. However, don't forget that you need to understand yourself to be understood. 'Just as no one is powerful without power or wise without wisdom, so no one loves without love,' said Marsilio Ficino. Understanding yourself can be a moving target if you do not follow any priorities or principles. My auntie, God bless her soul, used to confide in me when I visited her that she did not understand my uncle anymore, even though they had been married for more than twenty years. She understood him earlier on in the marriage but had lost track of who he was with time. The good thing is that there was a point they understood each other, and they would be able to revert to that if both were willing.

To understand yourself, you need to identify emotions that move you more quickly, that are stirred up easily without 'your' participation and result in a positive or negative reaction. You also need to understand the depth and level you go to when stirred, like the mimosa plant, which closes its tiny leaves when touched. Finally, you need to know how sensitive you are to some statements, words and actions. You will not find someone who will understand you instantly. If that happens, it should be a red flag, and you should proceed with caution, for it takes time to understand someone. You should look for someone with the foundation and cornerstones to building a solid, understanding relationship.

Listening and being listened to builds a strong understanding. You need to be a good listener and compassionate for any meaningful relationship to commence. You may ask questions like, 'Do you think I understand you enough?' to solicit more engagement, involvement and encouragement, which will draw out gaps that require bridging. The more gaps identified and bridged, the more you understand each other and the smoother the relationship. As I mentioned earlier, nothing stays the same. Understanding your other half is a continuously evolving process. For you to be compatible, you need to have similar genuine interests. I know of a couple who pretended to like each other's interests only to stop soon after marriage. Understanding each other comes from spending as much time as possible together.

The less time you spend together as a couple, the more a gap develops between you, leading to a split. Absence makes the heart grow fonder when you live separately before marriage. In marriage, absence is the road to splitting up. Put it this way, all applications we use on our devices require updating; if there is no auto or manual update, the slower and more frustrating it will be to use. Frustration leads to dissatisfaction, and you might even uninstall the app if updating has yielded unsatisfactory performance. Such is the fall away from understanding in relationships that results from less time together.

Understanding the other person is acknowledging their strengths and weaknesses, being there when your strength is required to neutralise their weaknesses and prop them up. They will be there when your weaknesses need neutralisation and propping up. Understanding the other person means knowing what to expect of them; it also means knowing that what you know about the person is partly correct, leaving room for the part you do not know yet. Finally, understanding means being happy with what you know and limiting your expectations. They are evolving, and so are you.

Understanding your partner gives you the means to nourish your relationship and make it more robust and lasting.

My generation and those before did not have the technology we have now. Meeting prospective partners involved going out to social gatherings. And chances were, you would meet someone with similar interests from your location who you already knew. Building a relationship from such a base was not that difficult; however, like everything else, there were challenges. The pool was not as vast as it is now. Parents encouraged starting a relationship with someone you already knew and used to say, 'The field of flowers is too enormous and unending; pick one and forget the rest.'

The old way did not require you to put your profile out on an app and market yourself, and there was no swiping left or right and no airbrushing of photos.

You would meet the physical person on outings; having said that, the matching process did not guarantee a long-lasting relationship, based on current statistics; there is not much difference when you look at the marriage to the divorce rate. In 2018, in New Zealand, the median length of marriage was 13.6 years (Statista, 2023). In the US, about 41 percent of first marriages end in divorce, leaving a good chunk of about 59 percent lasting forever. Finding your ideal partner, who you understand and who understands you, gives you the chance to be in that 59 percent success category according to a 2021 Goldberg Jones article on 'Divorce statistics: From the interesting to the surprising'.

You have a good chance of overcoming challenges in your first marriage than in a second or third marriage. The statistics say 60 percent of second marriages will end in divorce, which is quite a jump from the rate for a first marriage. After having a failed first marriage, you would think that the couple would have learned from the errors of their judgment in the previous marriage and would select a person who matched more closely the qualities they want. The need for a replacement probably leads to a rushed decision, only for them to realise that the second is worse than the first.

If you have had a failed marriage, you have a good chance of having a long-lasting second marriage if you find someone who has not been married before. However, you still have a good 40 percent chance of having a lasting second marriage even if you both had a failed first marriage. Therefore, selecting, learning and understanding each other's needs should not be rushed if you want it to last the long haul.

It takes a while to get rid of excess baggage from a previous marriage; if there is anything that you need to keep, it should only be the learnings and not a whiff of resentment, anger, frustration or disappointment. Those can get out of hand and soon dominate your thinking in your new relationship. It would be best to allow yourself time to grieve; a failed marriage is death to a creation that has been nourished, cared for and has reached its end of life. It is a creation that would have been part of your life, and losing that is losing part of your being. When you let it go completely, thank your ex for the learnings—that is the point when you can move into a new relationship.

According to the article, a third marriage attempt has a seventy-three percent failure rate; you have a slightly higher chance of maintaining or renewing a second marriage than a third. You notice that as one marriage fails, to get another that will be long-lasting becomes a more formidable challenge. In failed marriages, your choices lead you to the next partner. Who you attract is what you wished for, and what happens after the attraction determines the course of the relationship.

After splitting up with your mum, I looked for a place to stay while waiting and sorting out the divorce proceedings. The first advert I responded to was where I stayed for the next four months. When I went to see the site, Rey, the owner of the house, asked about my background, so I told him I was going through a divorce. That jolted him. I could see the word 'divorce' affected him. Then, calmly, he said, 'Maxwell, I have been married three times. I am single and sixty-five now. I have had some experiences and advice I will share with you. Welcome home.' *Wow! What is happening?* I thought.

What are the chances of finding a flatmate who has been married three times, who reads the Bible every day for guidance and is full of wisdom to share? When you are going through a divorce? Rey became the father figure I needed.

All events in our lives happen for a reason. The next person you meet will be in the position they need to be, for their benefit and yours. The universe connects and groups humans according to their needs and deficiencies. It allows us to learn from past mistakes and transmit those learnings to the neophytes. True to divorce statistics and studies, my new flatmate's first marriage was the longest, followed by two short ones.

Nevertheless, he was the right person I needed to guide me through the next phase of my life. 'Do not be like me and rush into the next marriage; take time to process your loss and heal. Blaming, anger, resentment, fuming and fretting will only lead you to bad health and perennial emotional pain and suffering,' Rey said.

I was looking forward to Rey's wise words each day come knock-off time. Then, finally, the otherwise tormenting journey became navigable. There was no divorce contest, and after four months, I moved out of Rey's house into my new place to start a new beginning. Rey begged me to stay longer, but I told him I wanted a place of my own where you, my son, would come and stay with me on weekends and school holidays, even though there was a family home that we opted to keep for your upbringing, and for Donovan, your canine brother's sake.

A year later, I dated someone for a month, and within that month, the lady mentioned marriage several times, which scared the wits out of me. I abandoned ship and ran for the hills. I was still raw. As Rey had said, I needed to heal completely. I thought to myself, maybe I need someone who has gone through what I did, married once or twice. My thinking had no basis in marriage statistics or studies then. I thought someone like that would work towards a long-lasting relationship. Three years later, someone who matched those attributes walked into my life. It was surprising how everything I had thought of in a woman matched.

Six months down the line, with the start, stop, start of Covid-

19 lockdowns, spending time alone and having conversations with myself, I began having flashbacks of the divorce experience. I told myself I was not ready yet, which led to the end of the relationship. My thoughts had delivered what I wanted, which is what the universe does. Whatever you wish for will be delivered in the way you want it. Maybe it was a trial to measure if I was ready to have another long relationship, but the test was unsuccessful or successful depending on how you choose to analyse it. Five years down the line, I am still healing. Some people heal fast, some take longer, and some never recover. Knowing the failure rate as I do now and the long healing process, I am so risk-averse at this point. In another year I will give it a go again. In the meantime, I enjoy the uninterrupted times I spend with you, my son.

Having a mum or dad replaced when they are still alive is not a pleasant experience for any kid. I grew up with both of my parents together. In my neighbourhood, I only knew of two families that had split up, and I detested the treatment of the kids by their stepmums. I never wished that on any kid, hence my hesitance to connect and start a long-term relationship. When I think about it, the kid in me tugs my pants and tells me it is inappropriate for your child to be as miserable as Clement, a youngster from my neighbourhood who was abused by his stepmother. Not every woman would harshly treat a stepchild, but the child in me keeps tugging my clothes and whispering, 'Do not do it yet, for the sake of your son.'

You are no longer a kid; you will be twenty-one next year, so I shouldn't worry about your safety in the home like I did when you were six months old. When you were six months old, your mum joined the police force, and she had to go away for six months of uninterrupted training in another city, leaving you, me and the nanny, who cared for you while I was at work. I still worry about you just as much as I did when you were six months old, though the nature of my worry has changed.

That worry will never fade, judging by how my dad worries about me even though I am fifty.

Worrying about our kids is what comes with being a caring parent. Being concerned about our offspring could be inborn or partly passed down through generational transfer. Granddad was the same and never stopped worrying about his many kids.

I am worried about your love life, and maybe I shouldn't be. But what parent wouldn't unless they have no 'relationship' with their kids? Sharing my life experiences will probably give you better tools to use in your selection process and comfort you when things are not going your way. I would not judge or blame you for your progress but offer my advice if you need it. Who you select and how you select them is entirely up to you, and I will support and embrace your choice.

However, always remember to be a good listener. People always want to be listened to, more so partners or spouses. Humans notice when they are not 'heard', when they are ignored, or their contributions are rubbished or talked over. Listen with compassion; listen with your eyes and your ears. Give them undivided attention and practise conversation generosity. Let them speak their mind without interrupting; humans lose inspiration to speak their minds unless it's confrontational. Do not water the seeds of anger and frustration by interrupting. Listening is respecting. Listen without prejudice and judgment. Give them assurance that you are there to listen and there for them. Listening nourishes a relationship, and you are both suppliers of this nourishment. Most of us rarely pay attention to others and their opinions if they are unwilling to listen to ours. Always remember that you get what you give.

Compassionate listening soothes and pacifies your partner's simmering agitation. Use mild language in your responses. My advice is there are no winners in domestic arguments. In trying to make your point and always win, unfortunately you're unintentionally harming the relationship by fuelling the next round of arguments.

See it this way, a relationship or marriage is like a game that requires both participants to play their part well to enjoy it, more like the recreational seesaw, with seating on each end. When one end goes up, the other comes down, alternating. When you want to win arguments in the relationship, you take the weight off the other and add it to yours until there is no weight left to play the game. It would be best to keep playing the game well, seeking mutually beneficial outcomes.

At the start of the year, I talked with my brother, Coster, who is two years younger than me, on WhatsApp. He asked my opinion on something I could not remember, and I went on to say what I thought. I continued to another topic, and then I stopped midway as I noticed something was amiss. Coster was always a talker as a kid and would not give anyone else a chance to talk. He'd even interject and answer himself, so I asked him why this quietness, then he said, 'Over the years and through the Bible, I have learned that we learn more by listening; I am listening and absorbing what you are saying. Carry on, brother.' I was impressed by his transformation. Life flows with ease when we listen with compassion.

Chapter 13

Let It Flow

Our minds are constantly poking and yelling questions at us as we traverse this plane of reality. Some are salient, and some are petty. We reply to their enquiries and concerns continuously. It makes no difference if the subject is about the person in front of you, the car you just passed or the one ahead of you, or the tasks you must do today. Your dinner, clothing, and social concerns are poking you, requiring your attention or consideration—as is your behaviour towards people and theirs in your presence.

We take stock, adjust and modify what defines us. A person you knew a while ago is no longer the same today. You can physically identify them with their name and appearance, but do not be confident, assume and conclude you have the old acquaintance's attention. Their mind will no longer be the same. Adjustments and modifications will have happened over time. If someone asks, 'Do you know that person?', rather say 'I *knew* him before', not 'I *know* him well.' You will never know another person well when you do not know yourself well. 'Partly know' can be close to a correct answer. You know what the person displayed in your presence, what was left out you do not know; what he thinks, and how he thinks you will never ever know.

Listening and nonresistance is a winning combination, Son, be it in yourself or your partner. Before I carry on, I am not saying you should be a doormat. I would not advise my son or anyone else to be a doormat but to listen first and resist having 'your way or no way'.

In our nature, we have resistance as part of our being, but all that we have, we can control. Resistance, yes, has unlocked opportunities for many a society, only as collective resistance. Individual resistance can be a challenge. However, it can only yield results if a strategy has first been crafted.

Over the years, I have seen a lot of stalled development due to impromptu, reactionary and unplanned resistance. Some political leaders believe they resist on behalf of their followers when they are only fulfilling their inner egos. I have seen careers that have stalled and died stillbirths due to stubborn egos. You may instead go about learning how to reach your final goal through persistence and nonresistance.

Water is the best example of an element with no resistance, but which wears away rocks and boulders and still flows with ease. A stream will develop in the mountains, flowing down, avoiding obstacles, creating its way. It can join with other streams to form a small river, which joins with other rivers to form the mighty Zambezi, even if blocked by a reservoir, the goal to get to the Indian Ocean remains; despite being stalled, the quest to carry on is diminished but never detached.

Yes, Son, you will face impediments along your way. If you do not have much power, you can ingeniously siphon your adversary's power by a nonresistant approach. If you resist a situation, it will persist, and being powerless can only mean more pain to you. You do not want that, worse if there is no clear end in sight.

Instead, this might sound counterintuitive, but the only way to rob another person of their power and ammunition is through blessing. Genuinely bless them, and you raise yourself above the thought of hate, which takes revenge and malice out of you. Nobody wants to fight someone who isn't going to fight back.

However, remain persistent in achieving your end target, whether it's domestic, sporting or political. The nonresistance approach does not mean you are defeated. It means you are above the thinking level of the other person. You can then detour like a stream down the mountain, and you will find a path that directs you to your destination, you will meet people placed to aid you. Every person on your way will be a golden link to the chain of your success, if you are persistent.

Sometimes, you will notice that the more you want to make your point, the more you face resistance and get challenged. Opposition often comes from misaligned opinions and beliefs, which are ignorant of the facts. It can, however, be a clash of personalities or fear of language, origin or racial difference. The more a person boasts, brags and gloats, the more resistance they face. The person might be in the highest office in the land, organisation, community or even in school; the opposition will always come and will eventually wear the person down. No level of punishment, harsh treatment, or even hitting someone's head with a knobkerrie, is capable of changing what is inside someone's head. If you want your point to be understood, know your audience and tailor parts of your points to resonate with them. Start like a stream or brook and weave your way, avoiding the opposition at the start until you gather enough momentum to cover them. Making a point is selling a point; salespeople do not disagree with a potential customer but instead agree while highlighting the benefits of what they are selling.

To disagree arms the opposition to their full capabilities; you do not want that if they have more mighty resources than you. But, on the other hand, to agree leaves them defenceless. Be as meek as Moses in the Bible but still reach the Holy Land, your objective.

An eye for an eye blinds both men, and a tooth for a tooth leaves them toothless. Likewise, kindness towards your adversaries incapacitates their zeal to strike. If someone forces you to go one mile, go with them two miles, and go with the flow; your motivation will generate the necessary energy to persist.

Nonresistance makes you lighter to lift, easy to recommend, and makes it easy to move on in any situation. It is easier to walk down stairs than up them. Being nonresistant does not mean being weak and cowardly. It means you possess the strength to refuse arguments and have better ways of reaching your objectives.

I used to like going out on Fridays to my local pub, The Barrel Inn, having one or two drinks while watching a band play.

The pub was packed to the brim when I walked in on Friday. I occupied an empty part of the table close to the front, two tables from the stage. Seeing people dancing and having a good time with a clear view of the band and the dance floor drew me to this bar. The vibe in the pub was always contagious, and it made you feel good.

There I was, having the lowest alcohol beer, nodding to the rhythm of the beat, smiling and greeting familiar faces; how I loved my Hoza Friday!

'Where are you from?' was the start of most conversations, as I was the odd one out. Depending on the mood, sometimes I would say I was from Howick, my neighbourhood, followed by a burst of gusty laughter after the person's reaction. Some would answer, 'Yes, I'm from that nation too,' while others persisted with 'Which country are you from?' On this day, this mid-forties, early fifties gentleman asked the same question, and I told him my origin country. He went on to ask how I had found the transition from being in the majority to a minority; I said that there was not much difference, avoiding a long conversation. 'I enjoy my Fridays just like back home, though the music is much different. But music makes people loosen up and dance, which is what I want,' I answered him.

Then the conversation shifted to his personal life. 'I'm here with my siblings and my daughter over there,' he said. 'We had a family meeting in the afternoon and decided to come to the bar to unwind. We are having a family disagreement. My family is giving me more responsibilities than I can handle. I have my problems to sort out, and they are piling more on top. I divorced a couple of years ago, and my wife got custody of our daughter, which I did not contest. I was happy with the arrangements, until she found that I had moved on and dated, then asked me to take full custody of our daughter,' he said. 'I told her that it wasn't an issue, and have taken her in for the past six months, and now she wants her back. I agreed, and I do not contest every request she has put in.' He paused.

'Good on you,' I said, 'if that gives you peace of mind. When we compete, we believe no one is walking over us. But the price can be astronomical to our mental and emotional wellbeing after a contest. It makes it easier if you know the person's history and intentions; back off and let them have their way; you lose nothing and gain your happiness and peace of mind,' I said.

'Thanks, brother,' he said.

'No worries, mate!' I replied, taking a quick sip of my beer.

'I don't know why I am telling you this,' he said, 'but I felt I needed to talk to someone besides my family.'

'Oh yeah, not a problem,' I said. 'Sometimes we need someone with a different perspective, and besides, I don't know you, probably we'll never meet again. Family matters will always get resolved; you will find a fair solution for everyone. Good luck,' I said, finishing my beer.

'Thanks, man,' he repeated.

Emotions are energy, and when you spend time focusing on a situation, your energy flows to the problem, and what you resist, you become.

My interest in American politics grows as the presidential elections approach, and I spend more of my leisure time watching news channels, switching mainly between Fox News and CNN. I have been doing this for as long as I can remember. Debates are the climax, and there will be no presidential election show like the last one. Trump must have spent his energy on the fear of losing to the worst presidential candidate, according to him; the more he resisted the idea, the closer the fear came to being fulfilled. 'If he wins, I don't know what I will do, and I will never speak to you again. I would have lost to the worst presidential candidate ever,' Trump said, referring to Joe Biden, addressing a rally in Wisconsin.

Embracing, acknowledging and respecting his challenger would have yielded a winning result. He was, however, breaking every universal law that governs humanity—a story for another time.

The weekend is almost over, Son; however, continuing with my nonresistance theme, Trump could have avoided disaster by focusing on his policies, past gains and plans. Humanity has evolved no matter how far left or right one is. When there are racial, ethnic, or tribal division, fear, wrath, and hatred get applied as political instruments, the candidate's chances of winning diminish.

Differentiate yourself from others by policies that envelop everyone, not by separatism. Spreading fear, anger, hatred and violence does not belong now; humanity has learned that in the past. Unfortunately, those who think they can gain leverage and prominence through dividing people are still employing that strategy but with disastrous outcomes.

As humanity evolves, two to five hundred years from now, the generations to come will probably know no country divisions or boundaries—all humans will live to enjoy their time in this universe, not as individual ethnic groups but collectively. No one would gain much by being only in their little corner of Mother Earth, their village, district, town, country, region or continent.

The modes of transport will be super-fast, and it will make no difference where you are and where you want to go. We have, as humanity, traversed continents *en masse*, now more than was ever imagined two hundred years ago. It takes a fraction of the time to travel from one corner of the world to another, compared to back then. Logically, the faster the transport system, the more people want to travel and the fewer restrictions they will allow to be imposed on them.

What happens after a two-country travel bubble gets created? More countries get added to the list, and there will be an increasing number of them, until there are no more borders. Humans are born explorers, and we are creators and do not stop learning. Accessing knowledge has never been easier than it is now. You can become a professional in most fields without entering the classroom or lecture room. The restrictions on improving yourself are slowly eroding. The more humanity gains new knowledge, the more the world improves and development accelerates.

When our time expires here, there is no memory stick, no memory bank; your knowledge is irretrievable unless you have used it during your existence—in the same way as money. It is only your legacy that remains. What you want to be remembered for is the question. If you have made billions of dollars, that cash needs to get used, you do not take it with you to the next world like the Egyptian Pharaohs used to think. Four thousand years later, their tombs are being opened and exhumed to reveal all the treasures they thought they would take with them to the next world.

As humanity, we've realised that the riches you accumulate on this plane of existence must be put to good use for yourself and future generations and not be buried with the dead for use in the next life. We can only embrace the present and be nonresistant, for change is sure to happen.

When the Wright brothers proposed constructing a machine that defied gravity, they met opposition from some groups who advocated for leaving air space alone, claiming that the sky was for the birds, the ground for humankind and the water for fish. Of course, variations of those opposition organisations will always crop up, but what is good for humanity will eventually prevail.

Allow yourself to be open-minded and let research lead and shape your beliefs.

The knowledge you have has come from other sources, me included, as we are not born with the innate ability to sustain us throughout our livelihood. It is dangerous to yourself and society if you believe your knowledge is the only truth and nothing else can supersede that.

Use the many varied sources of knowledge you have to track down the origin of any truths and contextualise them for relevance. Select what is relevant and discard the irrelevant and dross. You can't risk your life for a single person. Pick out what is pertinent and leave out the obsolete. You cannot put your life on the line for a thousand-year-old cause, like some religious extremists, believing that you will have a better life if the reason results in your death. You cannot continue fighting the departed's war. The way to resolve differences has evolved.

Your best life is right now. The past is gone, and you can only marginally control the future, a second, a minute, an hour, a day, a week, a month, a year, and on and on. A split-second error in judgment can turn your life belly-up. Control what you can see; variables are at play beyond your vision.

I know of a guy who had his career well-planned. He was hitting his milestones within his set targets. Milestones are necessary; always have them in your planning. However, the single steps take us to that milestone, and a misstep is all it takes to derail the whole plan. Self-control and self-discipline are the most you can control within yourself; without these two, your plan is a phantasmagoria, a mirage never to be reached, and your excuses will be bountiful. You will convince yourself to the point that your excuses sound real and legit, even though deep down, your subconscious mind will be telling you that you are only fooling yourself.

Missteps can come in various forms, leading to resetting milestones. Be wary of the words that you say as they may be the ones that come back to bite you in the behind in your hour of need. It is no longer your word against theirs now; it is your word against your word, as recordings are happening all the time. Do not fool yourself into thinking that any conversation with another person is just between you. Let it sit at the back of your mind that a recording is possibly happening that is retrievable, should the evidence be required.

In the same vein, if you notice a pattern and behaviour that is not worth tolerating and affects your wellbeing, speak out to the offending person or party and record the conversation for future reference. You can tell them that you record all conversations, depending on how fluid the situation is. In many cases, the mere knowledge that one is being monitored serves as a powerful deterrent. Most of the time, the wrongdoing ceases without further action.

Strength can come from weakness. The quest for power over others is a weakness in disguise. Know your options.

Chapter 14

Polish Your Diamond

Are you still gonna be talking about your second jobs, Dad? Junior asked.

Yes, Son, we'll touch a bit of everything since we have the long weekend to chill, I said. You see, when I start talking about stuff, I get carried away; it probably comes with old age. I sometimes wonder what I will be like in thirty years, I said. Grumpy, no, not me, if that's what you are thinking, I said laughingly.

Anyway, back at my second afternoon job, I was told the company had received another big order and planned to ramp up production in the tenth month of my contract. That meant increasing staffing as well. I was to get an assistant, who would help to relieve the added pressure. It was quite a relief to have some company in the stores. I listened to audiobooks in times of inactivity, which I immensely enjoyed, but nothing beats an actual person to converse with and share stories and ideas.

Aladdin was his name; he had worked for the organisation for more than ten years, having emigrated some twenty-five years prior. His story was quite like the rest of the employees; he enjoyed working for the organisation, liked the bonus incentive scheme and liked his work crew. I asked him which part of the world he came from, as I couldn't determine whether he was from India, Sri Lanka or Pakistan. And he came to my aid and said, 'Oh, I am from Sri Lanka; I came to this country as a student twenty-five years ago. There was a bitter armed struggle in my region between the

Tamil Tigers Liberation, a terrorist group, and the country's army. Many people got displaced, and I found my way into this country, which gave me security and a place to start my own family.'

'How nice. What did you do before joining this organisation?' I asked with much interest. Working with people from diverse backgrounds was golden, and I tried to get as much out of their experiences as possible.

Sharing past experiences and interests helps bonding with new work colleagues; I would not pass on this opportunity. Besides, he was a friendly chap willing to share his experiences. The more he shared his stories, the more I would reflect and notice some privileges I had overlooked in my life. We sometimes take for granted what we have in our lives until we meet someone who dreams of what we have and who nearly lost their life to have what came easy to us.

However, note this, Son, for whatever we get and have, we always pay the price to own that dream, financial or otherwise. Like how the Spanish say that God said, 'Take what you want and pay for it.' Those who lack your advantages wish they had them.

See it this way, Son: those who emigrate cannot take everything with them. A lot is left behind; they acquire all they can in the 'new' country but cannot replace those specifics they left behind. Those who do not emigrate will not have your new experiences and whatever you accomplish but will have what you miss. No one owns everything; what you lack in one area is compensated for in another. Life's journey has invaluable treasures no matter how much money you have.

Do not feel inadequate for lacking whatever you think is missing; discovering the gap instead should make you feel rejuvenated, for you have found your next challenge. Feelings of lack, limitations and inadequacy breed and multiply, only that. Nothing productive emanates from that thinking pattern unless you mentally transmute that lower form of thinking that pulls you down to a higher, more positive way of thinking.

Identifying and recognising a lack, limitation or inadequacy should propel you to achieve more. Some feelings disintegrate on their own if ignored. However, some keep recurring until you get to the source of them. Every event has an effect, and every development has a cause. The unwanted feelings of inadequacy are the effects of the cause. Find, if you can, the problem, the cause at the root of your difficulties. Release them out of your system. If the issues are still problematic, seek professional advice to get to the source.

I decided to wind up and exit my second job in my eleventh month there. Despite some feelings of inadequacy in my first job, not once did I think of relinquishing my role and finding a permanent position elsewhere or within FPH. Was it loyalty or realising that my primary job could eliminate the irritating crizzles, like transparent employee progression processes?

Sitting in a passenger seat while someone drives you on a route you navigate daily gives you the freedom to view and notice what you didn't know existed. You will have a different perspective; you will see the well-groomed flowers, the beautiful trees and the buildings. Stepping out of your routine into new settings makes you appreciate what you have.

A common saying in personnel management literature is, 'The best worker is the one you have.' You do not have to go to great lengths to find a great worker; you have them already. Familiarity breeds contempt, and I will add that we despise in others what we dislike in ourselves. When a nasty comment comes out, the anger and the hatred expressed is often evidence that the person who is hurting the most is the perpetrator. When you feel angry at someone, search within yourself to find the error in you, your inadequacy manifesting as anger directed at a poor victim.

We may move towns, countries, continents, jobs, or change partners, hoping to get a better version of what we have. But what we already have is probably the better version of what we will find, the difference being the extra bit of polishing required. The additional polishing requires a little bit of your input to get that desired finished product. An uncut diamond does not attract the same attention as a finished, polished diamond; however, a finished diamond has lost fifty to sixty percent of its size through polishing.

Prepare to lose through polishing before you get to the sparkling diamond. You have the uncut diamond in your possession; all you must do is shape it and use the diamond offcuts to cut and polish your final product, for a diamond can only get shaped by another diamond. You pay less for what you have polished than what you find already polished.

The adversities you face are the diamond offcuts that polish the final product, your improved self, your improved partner, and your better sense of acceptance in your job.

A friend of mine met someone she thought was her ideal mate, and all was going well at the start until there was an unevenness in the rate the relationship was growing. Her relationship milestones had shorter time limits than her partner's limits. Her expectations of support from her partner fell short. Upon discussion, the partner showed a willingness to grow into her ideal mate. But she had already decided to search for another, and nothing would shift. Finally, she told the partner that she believed there was someone with all the qualities she was looking for and walked away to find that one.

In relationships, there are entry-level qualifications and qualities you are expected to possess before being 'hired', like in jobs. If the entry expectations match, development begins for both parties. Letting go of a partner who ticked *most* of your boxes with the hope of finding one who ticks *all* your wishes is nothing but illusory.

No one will ever tick all your boxes until you have accepted the faults within yourself. To be fulfilled by another, you should already live a fulfilling life. The unmet expectations of a partner are limitations within yourself, which pull you back from progressing.

A person's fear of progress and weaknesses scares them when their partner exhibits those weaknesses. It is an insecurity that you can only address in yourself. One who has cheated has an intense fear of being cheated on; one who lies has an intense fear of being a victim of lies. So, someone who feeds their mind with worries is setting limitations for themselves. Have ticks in all your boxes before finding missing ticks in the other person.

Aladdin might have been happy with being part of the organisation, but when I asked him about his growth within the organisation, he gave me a picture of a ceiling that was low and hard to break.

The beauty of a building from the outside might not be the same from the inside; what we see in the front office might be different from the back office. The structure can also be beautiful inside and outside, only affected by poor furniture arrangement. What can affect the overall outlook of something can be minor issues.

Minor issues should not cause you to make decisions that involve significant lifestyle changes. Being patient pays a big dividend in the end; a drop in the share price of Tesla today does not mean the stock will fall off to nothing. If indications show a dip, there is no need to ditch it.

Seek relevant information, knowledge and wisdom from those

better equipped and experienced than you before you make a rushed decision. Reversal might not be possible. Pay for the services, if need be, as the price you pay now might be minute compared to the cost of a mistake or the cost of an already polished diamond.

You are the diamond. Never stop working on polishing yourself.

Chapter 15

Flying Under the Radar and Fear

Where we live, where we sleep, what we eat, what we watch, what we wear, what we drive, where we drive to, and where we work can be displayed to everyone. We, however, control what we put out for public consumption. The more you show your lifestyle, the more you attract interest and attention. Good for business, yep, everyone agrees, but not for your private life.

My coworker and friend JB has been working for more than ten years in the same role, a managerial position.

We had a lunchtime talk about corporate progress and development. He said his father in England taught him to fly under the radar as a kid. 'Do what keeps you secure in your role, and don't raise your head too high, for the more your head is above others, the more you become someone's target,' he said. 'The nail that sticks out more than others gets struck with the hammer first.'

I agreed. Those that rise quickly fall off the top soon if not fully prepared, or get transferred to places they do not like. It is good to challenge yourself, but only when you have those ambitions, hopes and aspirations. Look what happened to Mark, Robson, Jameson, Michael, Johan, and Ange—the list of co-workers JB had witnessed falling off their positions over the years.

Supporting his dad's theory, he had not been impressed by those rapidly climbing the ladder. They had all fallen off, and he was still secure and happy in his role.

Not boasting and bragging but still hitting the ball out of the park is a sure way of anchoring yourself to whatever position you are at and want. What cements your position is respect, dignity and admiration from your peers and critics. Movement from that position will only be determined by new needs or changes in your circumstances.

I love watching sports, be it on TV or in person when I get the chance. I love football, a sport with stars who do not shy away from showing the world how great they are. Celebrations demonstrate it after scoring—the chest-thumping, the summersaults, the sprinting towards the fans, the taking off the shirts, waving and showing off their six-packs—it's all the fun and glamour of winning but also ego-boosting for the players.

It would be boring without such antics. Some players remain humble despite an outstanding performance; they have very controlled emotions, and their performance statistics on the pitch speak volumes for themselves. Critics find no words for criticising them; foes and opponents see no reason to hate them. On the contrary, fans love them for their efforts on the pitch and for being grounded and remaining focused. They fly under the radar but remain in full view of the radar. One such player is Ngolo Kante, who played for Chelsea Football Club. Peers and opponents have come out to say it is hard to hate him; he respects his mates and opponents, and this is shown by his demeanour. He does not show off; despite earning millions of dollars, he doesn't drive the car of a top earner, but still drives his performance to the maximum when he is on the pitch.

JB's philosophy is like that of Ngolo Kante; he is there to perform his duties with precise execution but is absent in times of accolades; he doesn't like meetings but will contribute to solving issues. He only comes to our department social drinks, but not the companywide ones. He is mysterious to many outside the department, yet we greatly value him.

Both introverts and extroverts can fly under the radar. It is about controlling what you say and how you say it. It is about being where you are wanted, performing to the best of your abilities and limiting yourself from gatherings that do not add value to yourself but open you to criticism and unwanted attention.

For close to a year, I was flying under the radar at my second job. As much as people wanted to know who I was, I did a perfect job of diverting their attention to other topics if they became too curious about my background.

Flying under the radar is not, however, interchangeable with fear. Instead, fear is another mammoth animal of its own, which gets addressed accordingly.

Fear puts the world to a halt and prevents the progress of continents, countries, societies and individuals. Trepidation can be passed from generation to generation until one generation faces it and stops it dead on its path to the next.

For thousands of years, the Egyptians believed in an afterlife. They dedicated their lives to preparing for the afterlife. Where they were to get buried, how they were to get buried and what they were to take with them into the tomb was part of the planning. So be it ornaments, jewellery, cutlery, food and pets, though it would spark a furore from animal activists nowadays to kill pets for burial beside their owners.

The belief that dead people possess some form of omnipotence went on for thousands of years until one generation decided to check what life after death looked like in those tombs that had taken the pharaohs a lifetime to prepare, only to find mummified bodies and their loved possessions in the same position. The afterlife myth was burst open, it did not exist; no dead person possessed any superpower but was as motionless as the next stone unless moved by a living being. The fear of the deceased got passed down from generation to generation, and the new generation would grow brainwashed to the point that no thoughts of finding the truth existed in their mind. Generational fear is passed down through mythical scary stories and always with no evidence but hearsay.

That fear of the dead was not only reserved for Egyptians but most countries and societies. Unfortunately, that fear is still prevalent in some communities, in which people are petrified just thinking of the dead.

'Every cause has an effect, and every effect has a cause.' The cause of all fear is a lack of education or knowledge. 'Fear is a state of mind that has set limitations for its owner' (Napoleon Hill), a mind nurtured in lack and limitation stories.

In communities where darkness rules the night once the sun sets, you find stories passed from generation to generation that evoke fear in people. The worry here is darkness, which can be quickly taken away if you have night lights; the dark stories will not have the ally of darkness. Vampires, witches and goblins are stories that stem from the lack of light at night. Install lights, and the scary stories disappear as fast as the speed of light.

Fear is the threat of danger, pain and harm. You need to understand what harms you, guard against it, find resources to bar it, drive it away or avoid it altogether. For example, sharks can hurt you, but you do not fear sharks in the street or in your home because you understand where sharks live; you do not go to the beaches where sharks circulate, and the fear is gone. Lions are dangerous, but we do not fear lions in the cities or local reserves, only when we go on safari. We know where their habitat is. If you are not there, there is no fear; or you go with a tour guide and tour van, and fear is reduced.

Cars are dangerous but more so to those who jaywalk on the road or carelessly drive. We understand how hazardous cars are and avoid getting harmed, but we do not fear cars. Insecurity breeds fear.

My friend Jason had a lovely wife; he had been married for four years, going to five. You could see that now and then he would wear a worried face. It is not unusual; everyone gets sucked into their thinking at some point, which is visible to the next person. I do get into that state now and then if no one is around. I even get into a conversation with myself, only telling myself what to do, a one-way conversation. The more you acquire years on this planet, the more the propensity to give instructions to yourself verbally and mentally. I have known people who also engage their hands in these self-talks, and you can notice an internal conversation happening from a distance. I am not self-talking with gestures, but give me another twenty-five years, and it could be me. It is not a lack of people, friends or someone to talk with, but just self-directing.

Jason was a good friend, and we confided in each other. He had lost an income and was in the process of finding another job. He had two kids, not yet school-going age. His wife had been looking after the kids as his income was enough for them to live comfortably.

His termination package and savings were enough to last them six months without a job. Jason, however, revealed to me that he was afraid that he might not find a job that would give him an income like the one he had been getting and it might cause a lifestyle change for his young family.

'Look, you have a good education, a good profession, and an excellent job history,' I told him. 'No organisation will hesitate to hire you if an opening requires your skills. You have nothing to fear, Jason,' I said, touching him on the shoulder. Sometimes when we look at the downside of our situation, we fail to view the upside due to how heavily we have loaded the downside with cons.

We overthink, focusing more on the negative, like, how about the mortgage, the kids, the food, what if one of us requires medical treatment, what if this, what if that etc—leaving out the possibility of getting a job tomorrow or next week.

Hope should come from within yourself. Everyone else will be validating what you already know, and you do not need validation. If it does come your way, gladly thank the person. We should plan according to our needs and wants, not our fear. With anxiety, your plans are influenced by a 'fear super-spreader' with probably some ulterior motives.

Fear of not being feared and instilling fear to be feared is what despots do. It is a sign of insecurity massively proportioned. If you find yourself working under or with a person of this disposition, do not show fear, or you become their conquest. Instead, respect the person as you do to every other person. No one should fear another human being in the free world. When you fear another person, find the source of anxiety and insecurity within you.

You can feel insecure as a new immigrant, especially when a bully or despot notices your insecurity. No one comes and says 'fear me', but their actions invoke feelings of losing your job or some form of retribution. Knowing your rights will take away those fears. Educate yourself on the protection provided by the state or organisation, and the fear will fade away. Showing no signs of fear removes from a bully, despot, tyrant, or anyone of a similar disposition, the feeling of being in control.

Unlike the fear of darkness, the fear of Hell cannot be taken away by standard lights. It is unknown whether such a place exists other than what gets passed down from generation to generation through Bible teachings and other 'prophets'. One piece of the puzzle debunked is the reuniting of the body, soul, and spirit at some point to have a new life after death. If the three are to be reunited, the body will be entirely new—for one, you will have disintegrated.

That leaves the spirit, which connects the soul and body to the All, Source or God known by various names. The body cannot burn in eternal Hell or rise again, as it completes the earth's life cycle by feeding those that feed on the body the same as we feed on beef, chicken, fish and vegetables.

Should people be afraid of Hell? Absolutely, yes. But no one should be afraid of what will happen to the body after you die; as the spirit exits the body, so does consciousness. The Hell you should be afraid of is the Hell within you. You have Heaven and Hell within yourself. You have the choice right here and right now. The choices we make gives us peace of mind or a hell of a life.

Live righteously today, tomorrow is a precedent of today.

What frees you from fear is knowing how to live within the universal principles and obey them. Humanity, regardless of geographical location, understands these universal principles. Good and bad behaviour exists in society; we have the choices inherent in us. When you commit a good deed, you feel satisfaction within yourself. When engaging in an evil act, you can feel that too, within yourself.

'You will burn in Hell when you die, if you break any of the ten commandments' is what most of us were taught at Sunday school as kids. The combination of burning and death was a sure way of instilling fear in any child, and that fear grows up with you until you seek and find the truth.

Reward and punishment are still rooted in these teachings. There is a story about a preacher who was going from village to village preaching about Jesus Christ and salvation in Africa. When he started his preaching, he said, 'You all need to be born again, or you will go to Hell. No one had heard about 'Hell' in this part of the world. So, one asked, 'What is Hell?' and the preacher said, 'It is a fireplace where all those who do not believe in Jesus Christ will suffer and burn there eternally.'

'So does it mean all our forefathers, mothers and families who died are in Hell now?'

'No,' he said. 'You will only burn in Hell if you do not accept Jesus Christ when someone has preached to you about him.'

There was a deafening silence in the crowd digesting the last explanation; then the Headman said, 'If you had not come here, we would have been safe from the Hell you are talking about, yes? As we did not know about the person you are talking about, right?' There was a momentary silence again as it made sense to everyone, and even the preacher realised that he had put himself between a hard surface and a rock. 'You have come here so that those who will not accept Jesus Christ will go to Hell. In that case, you should not have come to my village.'

Even though the headman made the statements, the preacher's seeds of fear found fertile soil in the villagers' minds. Thus, the villagers needed rebirth to overcome the fear of going to a place of eternal fire, known as Hell. Many did convert as death and hellfire evoked far greater worry than converting.

Many people do not like giving speeches; to some, public speaking brings unbearable discomfort, also known as 'glossophobia'. Experts such as Heeren and others in a 2013 study from the *Neuropsychiatric Disease and Treatment* journal, estimate that as much as seventy-seven percent of the population feels pain speaking or speaking in public. In the household I grew up in, my mum was a disciplinarian, and from an early age, we were trained not to talk when visitors were in the house, whether the visitors were relatives or not. So being quiet was a sign of disciplined kids. You can understand her logic, since the eight of us are separated by a couple of years in age. So, if we had to start talking, the visitors would be drowned and overwhelmed by our loudness. However, the downside was that it led to a form of fear in some of us. The fear of speaking in front of strangers and visitors got tucked in our minds.

Our situation could have been different. But to keep silent when guests or elders arrive at the door is a common home rule that extends to schools.

Like, in my days at school, every class had a class monitor, who would keep order in class and write down the names of those making 'noise' or being talkative in the teacher's absence. Names of pupils who made noise in the teacher's absence got announced on Fridays for detention. To be safe, you had to learn to be quiet. That information got stuck somewhere in kids' minds, and as we grew up, we developed less confidence to speak in public. Even though there may be no link to the situation that first made us afraid, the fear implanted in the mind as a child overrules.

Finally, there is fear from ill preparation. If you are unprepared, or not entirely understanding the topic of the discussion, you will lack the confidence to participate fully and fear exposing your knowledge inadequacy. Self-belief overcomes fear only if you are fully prepared. You cannot become confident walking on broken glass with bare feet; however, your confidence level can swing from zero to a hundred if you are given protective shoes. The more prepared you are, the less fear you have.

As you move to expand your horizon, be it in business, work, sport or socially, it is normal to be a bit apprehensive now and then. Research, research and research until you fully know the topic you are to face. Then practise, practise and practise until you are confident in your performance.

You will be an impressive package if you work on not just your brain, but also your body and clothes. Fitness centres, or gyms, are everywhere and are affordable. Or you can have your workout session at home, which works well if you are disciplined. However, going to a fitness centre will give you the advantage of learning and practising new techniques. It will also allow you to interact and make new friends with like-minded people. There is nothing as confidence-boosting as having a body that you have worked on, shaped, and for which you have attained a set weight. However, do not feel less confident because you have not achieved your target weight. Please take it as a work in progress, which will add an exciting challenge to your routine.

Complement your physique by investing in some good quality attire. Your clothes should not be expensive but should fit you well and be fashionable enough to enhance yourself. Your brain, physique and clothes all wrapped in confidence will cause fear to scamper away from you and let you be a step ahead of fear in any public speaking situation.

When you suggested we join a fitness centre, I first thought you could go alone and do your workout. Still, you asked if I could help you identify exercises that suited you, to which I said a fitness centre instructor would be able to help you with that. Then I realised there could be a deeper reason than being there in the gym with you—the together-time.

Going to a fitness centre is not the only way to get into a body shape you are proud of; it can be watching what you eat, walking, running, yoga or whatever releases endorphins. The trick is to feel comfortable with your body, regardless of shape, size or weight. Not everyone is svelte in appearance, but anyone can be svelte in mind and carry their body oozing the same confidence as a supermodel regardless of height, weight, or size. Nobody is ugly, and everyone is beautiful, as we are all made in the image of the source, God. You are unique in his mind. You might want to tell yourself that you are one of one, that you are strong and fear *nothing*, when you have feelings of fear overcoming you. Telling yourself these things is the first step to believing them.

Fear of failure is one fear that most people have if they've passed through an education system that emphasised grading students according to achievements; more so if you were not gifted with an excellent memory. Education in the early years was all about memory retention. Examinations came in various forms: weekly exams, end-of-chapter exams, end-of-month exams, top-of-the-quarter exams, end-of-term exams, end-of-year exams and end-of-course exams.

In my primary school years, we were examined every Friday, and those who failed to reach the eighty percent mark would get an equivalent number of hits on their palms by the teacher with a thick stick named Cobra. It was so painful that no one would want to fail and get Cobra on their palms as a result. That bred a fear of failure from primary school right through to adult life. Failure to achieve the set grade was a sin punished by Cobra, imprinting red marks on your palms.

We fear not reaching targets that have been set by society for us, like getting married at a specified age, starting a family, buying a house, and on and on, and thus we also set targets for ourselves and then fear not reaching those targets. However, planning and preparation take away all the anxiety we may have towards any deadline selected for us or set by ourselves.

Years ago, I was lured to the popular stocks: lithium and cannabis. Most share market stocks were startup penny stocks that swung double digits from massive gains to massive losses within days. However, if you read the company prospectuses, some of these companies had the excellent potential to develop into large organisations. They would announce partnerships with offshore companies, developments in the pipeline, investments in research, and the progress of trials. So, it was alluring enough that I picked one of the stocks and bought myself a sizeable number of shares.

I would check a couple of times a week in the early days, which became once a week then once a month. The stocks were bobbing up and down, which did not bother me much. I again decided to check the performance more frequently. But towards the

Christmas break in November, I stopped paying attention to the stock. Then, end of March, after receiving the stock notification on my phone. I checked the performance, and boy oh boy, the stock had plummeted by more than seventy percent. I had lost seventy percent of my investment in that stock, and was I panic-stricken? No, I was not. You are only seventy percent down if you decide to sell. So, I kept the share stock and never worried about it.

There are two possibilities in the share market, lose or gain. First, we prepare for gains by researching using technology, bots, among other tools, which calms our nervousness and anxiety about losing money. Fear is thus minimised, not eliminated; fear is relative to experience and how much you know, be it in stocks, sports, business or work.

The more control you have of an outcome, the more negligible the fear; we fear what we do not know. Some suburbs are no-go areas in some countries, yet some people live in those suburbs. You would not expect people to live in those neighbourhoods if they are no-go. But only people who live outside the community fear the happenings in those areas; those who reside in the district have developed street smarts that protect them and their families from harm.

****

A while back, I got a Facebook notification of a friend request. I do not usually go on social media during my work period as it distracts me. Having coffee on my lunch break, I checked to see who had sent the request. In most cases, I delete the request if I check the profile and there are no photos of that person or no friends list to see. Upon reviewing this request, I noticed that Tapiwa, one of my close friends, was a mutual friend, so I accepted the friendship. Before I took the 'request', Facebook sent a warning notification asking if I knew the person. That was quite interesting as it was the first time I had been asked this by Facebook. Was this a new measure they had introduced so that you can only accept friends you know, or was it something else?

It aroused my curiosity, and I went on to accept the request. I got a messenger *ping!* in less than a minute. Twala, the new friend, had sent a 'Hi' message. I did not respond to the message as my lunchtime break was almost over, and I was not a fan of social media during the day. So, I left it for after-work time.

Mondays and Tuesdays are the busiest days for me. And this day was a Tuesday; I was doing the weekly reports. And on top of that, the end-of-year performance reviews were coming. Everyone whose evaluation had a basis on quality data wanted my stats; their performance bonuses would get impacted by the numbers that I provided, so I had to get the figures right.

Coffee keeps me going on busy days like these; I have a cup in the morning, a cup at lunchtime and a cup at 2:30 pm to finish the day. I completed the reports before 3:00 pm, which meant knocking off was 3:30 pm. I keep my phone on the charger during the day so that when I get home, I have enough charge to catch up on all that has happened while at work. My routine doesn't vary much.

When I get home, I have my dinner at 4:00 pm, shower, go on social media then read or listen to an audiobook. So, when I got to the social media part, I went on to reply to the message. But Messenger sent a warning again, which read, 'Do you know the person? Do not disclose your bank details to anyone or send money to someone you do not know.' Second red flag and more curiosity.

I wrote, 'I'm good, and you?' Then added, 'I'm concerned; why did Facebook and Messenger flag you?'

There was a momentary lapse, then she replied, 'It's the same as yours, so I am thinking...'

Then I texted, 'Okay, just curious how you found my name and what made you send me a request.'

'I know Tapiwa,' she replied.

Then I messaged back, 'Okay, from where? He is a good friend of mine.'

She texted back, 'That's nice, you live close.'

'Yes, same neighbourhood. Where do you know him from?' I asked. No answer came back, 'Where are you from?' I asked and got a quick reply,

'I'm South Africa, Johannesburg.'

'Cool, where in Joburg? Lived there for a while,' I texted back.

'Bedfordview bby, are you married?' she messaged back. *Another red flag.*

'Where in Bedfordview? I lived in Ells Park,' I replied, not answering her question.

'Bedfordview is not too far from Peoria,' she texted.

'Peoria' is probably a typo for Pretoria, I thought. Then went on, 'Cool, so what do you do?' I asked.

'I'm a business adviser; I also do part-time trading, and you?' She replied. *Another red flag*, I noted.

'Nice, how do you do part-time trading? Are there any meaningful returns with COVID-19 in the background?'

'Yes, sure. I'm an expert trader, but I do it part-time and occasionally now. I guide and teach people how to make successful trades.' That was a long answer, I thought. So, this must be the reason she was flagged. *Another red flag.*

I then messaged, 'Interesting, how do you guide making the trades? Do you choose stocks to buy for your clients?'

'All you need is your smartphone and your Bitcoin wallet. To avoid low signals or loss of trades, we use cryptocurrency for funding brokerage accounts; Bitcoin (Stock) preferably.' She replied, then she messaged again before I responded, 'If you don't have a Bitcoin Wallet, I'll guide you on how to open a Bitcoin wallet and begin your trade.'

'So how do you open the crypto wallet?' I asked.

'I advise you to use a Luno account precisely,' she answered.

'What is that?' I asked.

'Download the Luno app from your Google Play store; Luno is a Bitcoin wallet account,' she replied.

'So do I put money in that Luno wallet?' I asked.

'Yes, once you open the account, you will enable a few items to allow you to start making transactions on your account,' she messaged back.

'How much is the initial deposit?' I followed up.

'Doing trade is extremely profitable when using the right techniques and strategies. With as low as $700, you can make up to $2300 profit within three days of trading,' she replied. *Another red flag.*

'That is good returns, Twala; you must be a multi-millionaire,' I responded.

'I work for my company. Did you get the Luno app?' she texted back, and I sensed the urgency in her reply.

'If I put in the money now, do I get the returns in three days, by Friday?' I asked, whetting her appetite.

'Yes, you will receive an email once your trading section begins; trading begins immediately after depositing your money,' she replied. 'Profits mature for withdrawal within three days of your trading,' she added.

'So how are the stocks picked? Walk me through the process.' I pressed on.

'You will receive your profits in your Luno account,' she wrote, avoiding the question. 'Your bank account is linked too, and your profits go in for withdrawals.' Again, she avoided the question and carried on about profits.

'How are the stocks picked?' I adjusted my question.

'From the cryptocurrency market.' This time she replied. 'We use Bitcoin (BTC), to be precise,' she said. 'Once your stock profit is mature for withdrawal, it transfers directly to your bank account.'

Red flag, red card. Warning signs and warning bells were ringing all over; I had all the information I needed, my curiosity and questions answered. Facebook and Messenger had been spot-on in safeguarding their clients.

I went to my Facebook search button icon, clicked, and typed Twala's name on the friends' list. I clicked the three dots and chose 'block'. I went back to Messenger, and the message 'You blocked Twala's Facebook account' appeared. Then below, 'You can't message or call them in this chat, and you won't receive their messages or calls.'

Millions of people are losing their hard-earned cash through these social media platforms, getting catfished or lured with promises of high returns through dubious platforms and apps that might appear genuine but have bugs that siphon money out of your bank account. Navigating these terrains makes you the victor, not the victim. When I started messaging Twala, I had had a similar chat with a blocked 'Thabani'. Thabani had claimed to hail from my city but had not been flagged like Twala. It is past experiences that stop us from becoming prey, and it is getting under the rock that prevents the mice from becoming the eagle's lunch.

Knowing your territory gives you the confidence to navigate freely without trepidation, dismay, or apprehension. I quickly blocked Twala's account to protect my friends from her. Through friends is how the next victim gets picked. I would not have accepted the friend request if it hadn't been for a mutual buddy.

Six months earlier, at the start of the year, I had been targeted by a Richii Loidy, a mutual friend of my friend.

Before I replied to Richii, I established that he was from a religious community, as was the mutual friend. However, Richii was not as polished as Twala, as was shown by the first message.

'Hello sir, I'm Evelyn from Samsung company California USA' the chat started. The name on the Facebook page was Richii Loidy, and there she was introducing herself as Evelyn. 'Where are you from, sir?'

I replied, 'New Zealand.'

'Okay,' she replied, then asked, 'Have you communicated with any Samsung groups before.'

'Not sure; why?' I asked.

'Okay,' she replies. 'We have good news for you, sir,' she continued. The time was 12:56. I didn't respond.

'Hey.' Another message pinged in at 16:09. I didn't respond immediately. Then, at 18:02, I replied, 'I like good news.'

'Samsung company Ltd. We, the Samsung group of the company, formally want to congratulate you on your big win. A random ticket selection was lunch, and your profile got selected among the lucky winners. Thank you,' she responds.

I didn't reply immediately.

'You are among the ten lucky winners that won the sum of USD 800,000 from our company,' she continues.

'That is fantastic news. What will be the next step?' I asked.

'How do you want your prize money paid, bank transfer, or home delivery?' She replies.

'That is a large sum of money to do home delivery, right?' I asked.

'Okay,' she concurred. 'We will need your Full name: Phone number: Address: Occupation: Age: Bank name: Account number: For processing and registering your profile. Thanks.'

'Awesome, I prefer to have the money go to one of the developing countries where children are starving from lack of food; I think it's a good cause. What do you think?' I replied, smiling at my response.

'Okay,' she came back. 'We will need your Full name: Phone

number: Address: Occupation: and Age: For processing and registering your profile. Thanks.'

'United Nations have charities that are looking for donations, they will be happy to have that money, and you can note that it was an anonymous donor from New Zealand. What do you think?' I replied, enjoying the chat.

'Sir, you must put down your information right now, okay,' she messaged back, getting irritated. She then fired another message: 'So that we can deliver your prize money to you, sir, okay.'

'I don't need that money; I am a generous person, hence I want you to give it away, or you can have it in your bank account. What do you think?' I replied, anticipating another irritated response.

'Sir, this is a huge amount of money you won from our company,' she pursued. There was no sign of irritation in the response this time.

'Money flows into my account, every day, every minute, and this one that I have won, I am happy not to have it but give it away through a charity of your choice. God wants me to help the less privileged. What do you think?' There was no quick response. I had used her religious background against her to make her guilty. 'If you don't donate that amount of $800,000.00 to a charity, you will have a lifelong curse until you have done so. I represent my heavenly father, God, creator of the universe, and he has noted my pledge through you. The sooner you pay this amount to the charity of your choice, the better. If you do not, God will be punishing you every day,' I sent. That was the end of the chat, and she didn't text back. Two hours later, I blocked Richii Loidy's Facebook account.

Fear is like Richii Loidy; it may try to stick with you, but it will dissolve if you show that nothing is scary about its structure, which is real threats or imagined danger. Action on your part is all that is required to cure fear. Fear will rule your existence, and your offspring, and get passed on to future generations like a baton stick in a relay race without any effort. Fear will stop you from capitalising on opportunities. It will freeze and numb your tongue when your contributions are needed the most.

The last time I searched Richii Loidy's account on Facebook, there were no results. The Facebook account is non-existent now. Maybe the person behind it is living in fear of the curse since they were from a religious background. I hope the threat stopped the person behind the name from further harming people through identity theft and probably robbing them.

When you fear something, in this case, the curse, you will attract all that is related to a curse. And you will get confirmation from within yourself that you are cursed. A seed of fear can only germinate if the soil is rich and moist enough to support its growth.

For example, we have innate fears we come out of our mother's womb clasping, like the fear of falling. In some cultures, newly born babies are thrown up in the air to condition and overcome that fear. You always come to mind when I think of the fear of 'falling' and inborn fear, because I witnessed the fear you showed as a one-week-old baby while being bathed and how you clung to the edge of the baby tub.

We are what we are and where we are because we have prepared ourselves against fear. We have looked fear in the eye and boldly told fear not to bother us. We are continually protecting ourselves against the elements of fear and the outlets perpetuating it.

We are in the second year of the Covid-19 pandemic. The world has been in lockdown for most of these two years, borders shut; international trade has been heavily impacted, and so has productivity. It has resulted in minimal growth of the world's economy. Lives have been lost, and lives will be lost until we find a permanent solution to arrest the pandemic. The fear that gripped the world when Covid-19 was first detected is not the same fear that the world has now. The more information we learn, the less anxiety we have. It is the understanding of what harms or endangers us that allays our fears. Knowledge supplies us with the means for protection; protection minimises or eliminates the risk, and when we have control, anxiety dissolves. Fear can only remain if there are conflicting information outlets; just like in investment, research from reputable sources will give you correct or close to accurate information.

Chapter 16

Leader by Leading

Six weeks before Christmas break, I applied for an extra couple of days to have an extended break from my side job; I wanted to have the 23rd off but got told I had left it too late, so my application did not get approved, fair enough. In most workplaces that operate three hundred and sixty-five days a year, you must apply early for your application to be accepted, as everyone wants those days off.

I did not have any specific plans for the break. The music festival that I had in mind got cancelled. Winding down was all that was going to happen at home. It was not my turn to have a Christmas break at my primary job; we rotate taking Christmas breaks, and someone must go to the plant, check reports and release products for customers. It takes half a day to clear, and I would be out of the plant by around 1 pm. Nothing stressful.

With so much time on my hands, I could reflect on the past year.

I had been able to hold two jobs again for an entire year. We had renovated our rental house in Hamilton one hundred and ten kilometres away, driving to and from for four months and had done a remarkable job. For the five years I owned the property, the renovation plans had always been at the back of my mind, and with the 'Healthy Homes' legislation coming into effect the following year, ticking off this job gave me peace of mind. Struggling to get tenants is what I feared most in the house's old state, and the worry had gone after modernising everything in it. My stocks were tanking, but that did not worry me as I had no plans to offload them.

I came up with dates for when to give my notice at my secondary job during my break. I had gained the exposure I intended to get and witnessed and experienced the operations process. I had made new friends, lifetime friends. So, when we got back after the three-week break, I went to the administrative office to let them know about my intentions.

I gave a six-week notice, not that it was a requirement; two weeks was the contract notice period, but since I had developed a cordial relationship with the team, giving them enough time was my way of thanking them.

Roxana, the HR lady, said she was about to ring me when I entered the office. 'Your manager wants you to attend some training; I wanted to check on dates that suit your availability,' she had said. I told her that I had come to the office to let them know of my resignation and notice period.

I told Roxana that I had a project that would require more of my afternoons, as well as my primary job. The plan had been to work for six months, as per the initial contract, since I had a primary job.

She told me to come back in the last week of the notice period to fill in some termination forms.

It was a five-minute walk from the admin block to my workstation. My supervisor, Mohan, got rung by Roxana, so he knew that I had resigned before I got to my workstation.

Questions were going to arise, and I was expecting that. I got a funny one: 'So, what are you going to do? Are you going on benefit?' asked Tim, one of my team members.

'No, Tim, I enjoy working and earning. I would not quit a job to go on benefits,' I told him

'Have you got enough savings to sustain you and your family?'

'Have you got another job?'

'Are you going to come back?' A barrage of questions came at me.

I said, 'Guys, I am still here for the next six weeks. I will be able to answer all your questions on my last day. You can ask me any question you can think of then.'

I told Mohan I had been planning to write a book for a while, and I had decided to do it this year, and it would need my afternoons. He said the job was here for me if I changed my plans.

The following day's afternoon shift, when I clocked in, I saw Rod, the Manager, by the store entrance. He smiled and said, 'Good afternoon, Maxwell. I heard you will be doing something exciting. What is it?'

I said, 'Oh, it's something that I have been sitting on for a while, and feel this is the year I must do it—I will be writing a book.'

'Wow, that's exciting. Can I get a copy when it's published?' Rod said.

'Oh, for sure, you will get yours signed by the author,' I said jokingly.

'What are you going to be writing about?' Rod quizzed.

'It will be about my experiences after moving into this country, work experiences mostly, including this organisation,' I replied.

'Hope we gave you a good experience,' Rod responded.

'Your organisation's standards are way above everyone else I have worked for, and that is no lip service,' I commented. 'I am impressed, and thank you for having me on your team,' I told him.

'If you feel you need a bit of a break from your writing, let us know, and we will organise something for you,' Rod said. 'Also, if you need any help with your book, let me know, and we can help you.'

You can only get comments like that from a confident representative of an organisation who knows there is nothing to hide in the organisation's running, no unethical goings-on. A representative who believes and practises the embedded respect culture that cascades from the top down to the shop floor. Every worker will become an ambassador of the organisation if they get treated with genuine respect. Workers mirror their leaders, and leaders reflect their thinking, and their thinking becomes the culture of the organisation they lead. Change the thinking at the top, and automatically it changes the thinking at the bottom.

Sarcasm is something I never encountered at FPH. In Rod's leadership, the stores department starkly contrasted with my primary job, where some managers were known for humiliating subordinates for all to see. Blaming was the order of the day.

Blaming comes from an unmet expectation, which comes from a faulty mapping process. These are the effects of a poor process design designed by the leader or with the leader's input. Then the blame gets entirely levelled at the poor soul at the other end of the chain. Wise leaders would ask themselves, 'What did I miss that I passed on to poor Jack to make a mistake?' instead of attacking, belittling, and taking away Jack's dignity.

'We still have six weeks with you; I will see you,' Rod had said, as it was time for him to go home.

'Thanks, boss,' I said as he walked out of the stores. Rod did not demand your respect as his subordinate, but he earned it. Genuine care is hard not to reciprocate, regardless of your position in society. It becomes bidirectional; you give respect. It returns to you in the condition you have delivered it. See it this way: the respect I give you as my son is the respect you give back to me, your dad. If I disrespect you, you will disrespect me; it might not be visible, but it manifests as resentment.

Always remember, Son, every human deserves your respect. Do not fight other people's wars, and do not let others influence you to prejudiced thinking about others. A misunderstanding between two is for those two to resolve, not for you to judge and fuel the fire. You have your journey and life's tasks to accomplish, rather than a misunderstanding you are not part of, unless you can take a neutral approach to help resolve the issue.

Back at my primary job, my manager Pete spoke of early retirement every now and then; it had become a song for him. At the start of the previous year, he said this would be his final year of employment with the company. Pete, just like any human, had his strengths and weaknesses. He avoided long talks most of the time as he knew I had ready questions for him. He would peep into my office, have one or two words and go to the next office. His retirement was imminent, but the succession plan was as clear as mud. Every time I asked him the question about my position in the chain of succession, he would say it was not for him to say who moved to which job, as he was leaving. On one occasion, I told him, 'You might be going, but your opinion is valued and still carries weight.'

One answer I got was, 'They want to see your next move.' Who are they? What move? Lots of questions that needed answers.

Then one morning, he walked into my office and said, 'I have submitted my resignation. I am finishing on the twenty-sixth of February.' Finishing *when*? I thought to myself. What does this mean? His last day at work is my last day at FPH, my second job. Is it a coincidence? Is it a chain of events preset for me in this life's journey?

It was futile to ask about changes that would happen, as they were closely guarded secrets. When succession planning becomes a secret, that's a good indicator of a process not aligned with the purported culture and principles of the company. This reminds me of an incident that happened more than a while back when the regional team visited the plant and audited the processes. I got told to go to the Plant Manager's office, which was unusual. On my way, my mind filled with a flurry of questions. Had I done something wrong? Had I said something to someone out of line, had I commented about something? Worry, worry, worry went through my head on my way to his office. I found four other co-workers from different departments in the office, all recently employed and new immigrants, all wearing the same worried look.

Then the Plant Manager said, 'There is nothing to worry about, guys; the company will be audited in the next couple of days by the regional team. I need your help to give the auditors positive feedback. We have selected you to be the auditee, so you will be called in when your time comes to answer and respond to their questions. Auditing will be happening here in my office, but I will not be present. I trust you will help us lift our scores above other plants.' He was the same guy whose every second word was an F-bomb in meetings.

No matter how the auditors tried to rephrase the questions, the answers they got from each of us were positive. Who would give a negative answer not knowing what would happen after the auditors were gone? New immigrants and an intimidating environment; only the rehearsed answers were the outcome. The residual culture of those days may reappear at some point if left unchecked.

Victoria, Pete's assistant, would take over. Other than that, everything else was kept under wraps.

Victoria was a bright young lady who valued respect foremost. I welcomed the change... No one worked as hard as she did. Vicky, as we called her, breathed work. She had the philosophy of going the extra mile. No one deserved that position more than Vicky did. I backed the decision and promised to give her all the support she required, which I always do to whomever needs my help, and so should you, Son. For you do not know when you may need the same support from them. If it is not returned, do not be discouraged, for you played your part; help will come from another source to compensate you. This also applies to our earnings. We earn according to how we value ourselves. We can keep searching until we get paid what we are worth. If you do not receive what you are worth, the universe has a way of fully compensating you through other methods. No individual or group can withhold and take away your worth forever; their actions or inactions will always catch up. That is how the universe revolves.

Care and support are reciprocal. Nevertheless, the secrecy around the succession gave me concern about negative elements of the work culture. Internal notice boards are a good starting point if you want a view of an organisation's processes and values. Updated news always gets posted on these boards. I used to stroll by these boards and read the daily organisation updates. On one such reading, I came across a notice on electric vehicles. There was a loan facility available to workers interested in buying electric vehicles at reduced interest. As an advocate for combating climate change, the company supported the cause in every possible way, down to the shop floor worker level. In every car park, there were charging stations for electric vehicles. Only electric vehicles were allowed to park in those parking spots. An impressive initiative.

I wondered how many companies had installed, or were installing, charging stations for their employees. I only knew of FPH and the Sylvia Park shopping mall in Auckland, which had such free charging stations for electric vehicles at that point in time. Some organisations set standards, the 'pacesetters', but are not vocal and let their ambassadors, the workers, and the results do the talk for them. Then some organisations, the laggards, are too vocal and talk over their ambassadors, the workers and the results. Their reputation gets obtained through their workforce and results, not their website. One of the share stocks I have given up hope on is a company in the medicinal cannabis industry. It lists itself as a driving force in the industry. It has eye-catching graphics and uses colourful language in its announcements. But that's all it is, fuelling hope and the promise of growth to shareholders. Unfortunately, the share price keeps pulling in the negative direction despite what the company says, quarter after quarter. Which is why integrity is more valuable than share price because it fosters trust between shareholders and the organisation, which eventually increases stock value, all stemming from mutual respect born of honesty.

Most people get into business for one of two reasons: making money, or making a change that improves humanity for a fee. However, there are other reasons, such as being your own boss, doing what you love and calling the shots. Beyond that, be and remain principled.

Life as a worker is a constant grind, whether you are a shop floor worker or a manager, the difference is in rewards, but it is still work.

Identify a gap, an opportunity that allows you to generate money. Options are all over and no longer governed by borders, regions or continents. Work to raise capital, set a working period for yourself, set a financial target and save to meet that target, cut unnecessary expenses, buy value-appropriate assets, and gain equity. Buy a good car that will last you more than ten years. A vehicle can drain your savings. Avoid the urge to change cars. Avoid brands in your saving journey. The time will come when you can buy whatever you want.

Avoid friends that do not share your values. Avoid friends that encourage spending rather than saving, in your quest to reach your target. I keep coming back to you and your friends, and I think it's because as you grow up, some of your decisions will be or can get influenced by the company you keep, your friends. We spoke about it so many times from when you started skating with your friends; now that you are a bit older, it might be time to stop talking about it. I think the message will always be the same but spoken differently. I am over fifty, and my dad, who is just over seventy, still sends messages to me now and then to remind me to be careful with people I associate with; you are an average of the people you spend most of your time around.

I still respond to him the same way I did thirty years back, that he does not have to worry about who I associate with as I always try to have good people and friends around me.

Have time with yourself if there are no good friends to talk to, as the best friend you will ever have is yourself. When you are by yourself, do something that develops you so that the next time you meet your friends, you will be a better person than the last time you were together.

'Do not allow yourself to be a conduit of other people's frustrations toward others. Your values and principles should not be diluted and changed because of your position in society, work or business.' I woke up to these messages on my WhatsApp one Saturday morning from my dad. After reading the text message a couple of times, I said, 'Sure, Dad, those are wise words; I will pass them on to your grandson and my friends.'

There are angry and cunning souls full of malice in society who would use you for their selfish needs if you are not careful. They identify a particular target whose character they want to tarnish through bullying, then they recruit you to do their dirty work. They stay off the frontlines, out of harm's way, by transferring their anger onto you, and feeding and encouraging your hatred and resentment. You then end up feeling their level of anger towards the target, and eventually, you execute their plan. It happens in workplaces, in politics and in business. If you allow yourself to be manipulated in this way, you will eventually bear the full wrath of the suffering when the tide reverses. The agitator knows the tide will turn, and they use you as a shield for their devilish behaviour, avoiding the full weight of the consequences.

Chapter 17

Mission Final Days

Sometimes, we get drawn back to a place, person or situation, and we can't figure out why it happens that way. I know of a friend who had a boyfriend she would walk out on one day, and then she would be back a couple of days begging him to get back together. I know of a friend who left his country, so disappointed that he said he would never come back again, only to return years later to settle. I know of a person who constantly complained about the company he worked for but ended up clocking forty-five years of service in that same organisation.

Every place or situation we are in is an opportunity to learn and grow through experience or observation. All we need is to open our eyes, ears, and minds. Sometimes the revelation and realisation come to light after leaving a scene, a minute after, an hour after, a day later, a month later or years later. It may come as what sounds like regret, but regret *is* learning. Coming up with an alternative method or decision is a remarkable achievement, and it is the effect of learning.

I met a lady one Friday night at my local pub, The Barrel Inn, and we talked about relationships. She opened up and shared her past experiences. She had been through three unsuccessful marriages, which she blamed on herself. She still wished to try again for the fourth time, but she said, 'I keep making the same mistake; I never learn. Family and friends have advised me, but I keep falling for the wrong guys.'

'You know your weaknesses from the sound of it,' I said. 'You probably need to make a complete turnaround from those attributes you attract by creating a new list that will guide you. Whatever you have identified needn't be part of your future conquest. However,' I said, 'You may want to know if you didn't know already that what you have identified as your main weaknesses are your strengths. You are attracting what is the opposite of what you need and want—in doing so, you can identify what it is you do need, but you are failing to adjust to those requirements...'

It is hard, or next to impossible, to change the other person; it is a futile attempt that leads to frustration and giving up, as you have experienced in your case. A person can only change if the change agent is within themselves, not forced upon them by another in a relationship. People change when the change gets instant rewards. And people degenerate into their old selves when benefits come in dribs and drabs. However, the glue that binds the two together needs constant replenishing before the adhesive weakens.

Being attracted to someone means the pull is stronger than the push. But the degree of movement by the other person determines the 'point of contact'—the point at which the relationship ignites.

Retreating to your zone, after the 'point of relationship ignition' (the attraction) expecting the other person to follow you, only works if they want to move from their point. If the other person refuses to budge, you either must move back to that point of contact yourself, or there will be a gap in between you that will reduce the ignition, and eventually there will be a complete detachment. Some conversations can happen, but conversations are just conversations; they are only words that come out after filtration and editing to match the expectations of the other person but not always the inner self.

Be convinced by deeds, not words; words are a means to an

end; words are transitory, filling the gap before the action, and the action should not take too long to commence.

Suppose you keep coming back to what you want to let go of. Search deep down within you; there is something worth salvaging. Something that pulls you back, and something that is yearning to be rescued and discovered. There is a rough diamond that needs polishing. Understanding and knowing yourself first is required to complete the circle. It is not a weakness to return to your accustomed grazing patch after you realise that the green grass you saw from a distance was nothing but illusory or required more to chew than your teeth's capability. How you come back hinges on how you left in the first place. You can only burn your boats like Julius Caesar if you are sure of victory but never your relationships with your relatives, for it is those relations that will bless and uplift you wherever you are in this universe. The human connection created at birth and the connections you make along your journey are unsevered. Some humans will leave large imprints on you, some minuscule, but revere all, as those with minute impressions might come back to continue from where they exited. Embrace their return, and help them in every way possible way to resettle again.

****

As my notice time at FPH drew close, I grew nostalgic about the location and its people. I thought of those with whom I had had a joke, a conversation, supper at the cafeteria, a stroll to the café, shared chores, or who had assisted me in settling into the position, encouraged, motivated, smiled at me and nodded kindly. These were the kinds of memories I would remember for quite a while.

Workmates are what make our jobs enjoyable or miserable. You might be introverted or extroverted, but either way, whether there are workmates, and how you interact with them, will affect you, positively or negatively. I exchanged phone numbers, Facebook invites and Messenger details with those who wanted my details.

A couple of days before my finishing off day, Mohan, my supervisor, informed me that we would have a shared dinner as a department. The company had given him a voucher to use as a farewell token. 'It is pretty humbling,' I said, as I was not expecting anything like that at all; I had been there just shy of a year. And in my other workplace where I was permanent, the company would not contribute anything to someone leaving within a year of service.

My boss at my primary job, Pete, was going on early retirement in a couple of days. Victoria came to my office that morning to ask if we could contribute some money to buy Pete a present as he did not want to have a big gathering on his last day. He had thirty-five years of service with the organisation, had been the Quality Manager for more than five years, and liked interacting with all the staff. I told Vic, 'This is unheard of; someone with that long service can't just slip away without a farewell from his workmates—we need to do something for him.'

Then Vic said, 'No, Pete has already told the boss that he doesn't want any gathering, and no convincing would change his mind.' We eventually concluded that we would have a surprise farewell for him then, despite his objections. I contributed twenty bucks for finger food. Vicky collected a sizeable sum from staff to buy a present, and the company eventually chipped in with food.

'A good surprise it was,' Pete acknowledged in his farewell speech.

That morning, we had Pete's farewell at my primary job, and in the afternoon, I went to my farewell at FPH. The break was at six, and an hour had been reserved for the goodbyes and the food. There was a variety of finger food and plenty that remained unopened and had to be carted back to the cafeteria. My surprise was getting a shopping voucher for fifty bucks from Aladdin. I had worked with him for only a couple of months, and he gave me a fifty-dollar coupon. What a great example of a human he was. It flashed in my mind that I had given Vicky twenty bucks a couple of days ago to buy a present for Pete. And here I was holding twice the amount I had given out. The universe works in mysterious ways. Like I always say, Son, be a good human being, be generous, help those that need help. Of course, not everyone will come seeking your assistance. But you will know when someone needs your help; put yourself in the shoes of that less fortunate person, and you will feel what they are going through—the uncertainty, the anxieties, the unfulfilled dreams, the frustrations, the pain, the suffering.

Generosity does not have to entail financial contributions; time, advice, physical assistance and advocating on a person's behalf are all ways to be helpful without expecting anything in return.

Chapter 18

My Brother's Keeper

A couple of months after Pete's retirement, Vicky, the new boss, came into my office on a Wednesday morning and asked if I had seen the invite for our department's monthly safety meeting scheduled for the following week. I said I had, and I accepted the invite. Vicky went on to say that the department was about to undergo some adjustments. One of our team leaders, Oka, had given his notice of resignation. 'Since his last day is the following Friday, if we hold a safety meeting, we can combine it with a farewell for him,' she spoke. 'And may I also ask you to chip in so we can purchase something to eat and share?'

I wondered why the sudden decision. Had something happened that he was not happy with to tender his resignation? She said Oka wanted to buy a house for his family. His wife had been living in Tonga for the past ten years, looking after their ageing dad, and they felt it was time for the family to live together. The only way he could raise the deposit would be to resign. Then he would access his superannuation contributions. However, the organisation would not facilitate accessing his superannuation contributions without him quitting.

'That is wrong,' I said.

'I know. You can get your KiwiSaver contributions to assist, but you can't get our company retirement fund,' Vicky added.

When we bought a house a while back, I recalled going to the HR department asking if I could leverage my superannuation fund contributions to put down a down payment on our first home. I got advised that the funds were not for purchasing a first home. Assisting first-home buyers was not one of the fund's benefits. The superannuation fund would only help if your existing residence was about to be foreclosed on, owing to financial difficulties.

That was a sticking point for me and did not make sense to someone trying to get on the property ladder. *The fund benefits need changing*, I thought to myself as I left the office disappointed. After your mum and I managed to put our other savings together and raise the deposit, I put the thought to bed. The house prices were not as high as they are now, and the deposit required was only five percent, which was reasonable. Five years later, Lionel, one of my workmates, came to tell me he had submitted his notice as he wanted to access his superannuation fund for a home deposit. He was so distressed that six years later, I could still visualise the contours of his sad face narrating what HR had told him. 'I got told that the company is not a financial institution that lends money—I must go to the bank.' That was the harshest statement I had ever heard from an organisation to its employee. I consoled him and wished him the best, as he told me he had a job lined up already. Although that's not what Lionel wanted, he had no choice.

Now Oka was in the same position and about to leave the job he enjoyed so much to buy a house for his family. Nothing gives you security more than having your own home and secure employment. Being forced to trade in one for the other is cruelty that should not be allowed if there are alternatives. Oka came into my office an hour after Vicky to confirm the news of his imminent departure. 'I have tried all I can, my brother, to ask for help from the company and still got told, no, there is no alternative other than to resign. They might employ me later, but I must resign for now. Can I have your email address to continue making my contributions to our Lotto syndicate?' That was like a dagger piercing my heart, and I felt helpless. Oka had been a member of our Lotto syndicate for the almost ten years he had been in the department; every week, we gave each other hope and laughed that this could be the lucky week for us. It was part of being a team. Vicky joined the syndicate the previous year as she said she would be left working alone if the alliance won; it was all about being part of togetherness, *ubuntu*.

I gave Oka my email address while working out in my head what steps to take. This needed to be changed, I thought. The superannuation fund is to help with retirement, but so is the KiwiSaver fund. Although both have shared objectives, if the KiwiSaver can assist first-home buyers, why was this fund unable to do the same as the KiwiSaver? *How is it like that? When did the benefit lists get drawn? Where was this drafted and who drafted and passed the benefits list?* If you had had access to my brain, you could have observed billions of neurons working overdrive, receiving and sending commands to develop a solution; Oka needed helping. That's all that was in me; I had to do something. I am my brother's keeper; his pain is my pain.

On lunch break, my routine is to read news updates. I decided to forgo that and research how to make a superannuation fund complaint. I found a fund product disclosure statement and the PDS 'complaint process and procedure'. The information I found gave me hope. What I needed now was to find an updated member booklet. The one I had gotten from the fund providers was outdated by six years.

After finishing my reports, I emailed the HR personnel, Linda and Ava, asking about an updated version of the superannuation member booklet. I did not get a response for the next two hours, then I rang to make a follow-up, but there was still no answer. I waited another hour and still got no reply or call back, my brain working on overdrive for a solution.

I decided to call the providers and ask if a situation like my colleague was avertable, if there was a way to access his money without termination of employment. I introduced myself, my name, and where I worked and told the person that as a member, I wanted the benefits list of our superannuation fund changed as it no longer served all its members' needs. It does not make sense for anyone to resign in order to access their contributions for a deposit for a first home buy. I asked the Fund Manager what I needed to do for that change to happen. He said everything I said made sense, then added, 'Your colleague's case got discussed yesterday, and a solution was found that so he can access his contributions without leaving his job. I spoke to your HR team this morning; he needs to go there if they haven't contacted him yet. He will need to fill in some forms to start the process. I assure you it was a positive outcome, and he needs to withdraw his resignation.'

After our conversation, I was so pleased with the development that I rang Oka to tell him that things had improved, which was the most pleasant news he could have dreamed of. He loved his job, and his anguish had been so raw that it had infected everyone he encountered. After his lunch break, he walked into my office, puzzled and happy.

I congratulated him and asked if HR had contacted him yet. He needed to withdraw his resignation and speak to the boss. I felt relieved and delighted, as if I was the one getting the assistance for buying my first home.

Oka said he had been notified of the good news just before I rang and had also withdrawn his resignation letter. The next step was to fill in the forms and contact a mortgage broker and his bank to get a mortgage, as he now had the required deposit. So, he was on his way to buy a home and bring his family together after living apart for so long. Nothing gives joy more than seeing your colleague's happiness after getting through anxious times. His whole situation changed from a gloomy future to a more secure lot. After sharing our joy, he returned to his workstation, and I carried on with my daily tasks.

Soon after Oka left, I got a reply from the HR personnel with an attached member booklet, last updated five years prior. Unfortunately, the office bearer whose name was on the brochure had left the company—the benefits list and booklet required updating every year by 30 June. It was out of date, my intuition had been correct.

I was happy for Oka and the outcome but still felt that I had to do something to guarantee a positive result for the next person after Oka, who would need the same facility. As I walked to the warehouse to check some packed pallets that needed my attention, I couldn't stop thinking of how I would get the attention of more stakeholders in the superannuation fund who would share my views.

When I got back to the office, I followed the advice of the fund representative and the information I had gathered from the fund managers' website for raising a complaint. It was going to be an internal complaint as a member. That's how I was framing my next move. I could do that without jeopardising my employment. I would copy in the employer and the fund manager, noting the sticky issues I needed to address. Oka's situation was favourable; why were other cases not addressed? How many others got addressed? What factors were used to make this decision? Why not use those criteria as blanket criteria for all first-home buyers and amend the benefits list, and let the whole workforce know about the development? For present and future HR personnel, this would make the benefits list clear and straightforward to understand, and it would respond to members' needs.

I wrote an email to the superannuation fund representative, Mackay, and copied in the company director and the HR team.

Hi Mackay,

Thank you for the fruitful discussion we had this morning regarding accessing superannuation funds for buying a first home. Repeating my thoughts, I think some amendments should be made as to how the fund best serves the needs of its members, which should mirror or be better than the KiwiSaver Fund. A lot had since changed when the benefits list got amended, e.g., house prices rocketing.

Members do not have to resign from work to access their contributions to buy their first home like [Lionel], [Fermi], or [Oka Mani]. He tendered his resignation yesterday, through the advice he got that resigning was the only alternative to access his contributions. Hence my contacting you.

KiwiSaver Fund and [our company's] Superannuation Fund serve the same purpose, so they should be when buying a first home.

The benefits for members should be stated and concise, including the *availability of funds for first-home buyers*. Oka Mani's case got a fantastic positive outcome, but what about the next member?

Who would need the same facility? Would they also have to write a resignation letter for the case to be given the required attention?

[Our company] needs to include accessing funds for first home buyers as a case for discussion and an amendment is required to existing member benefits.

It might be a long process, but can you forward my suggestion to the team that makes decisions for the fund.

Thank you.

Kind regards,
Maxwell Mkoki
SUPERANNUATION MEMBER

I sent the email just before I knocked off and expected a response that afternoon or the following morning. Instead, I did not get a reply until after 10 am the next day.

Vicky entered my office and shut the door behind her as she said she and I needed to have a serious talk. She surprised me; I'd been thinking about the end-of-year review process that needed finalising, and the deadline had passed without her comments. I assumed this was going to be the talk. She sat in the only visitor's chair in the office facing me and then said in an interrogating voice. 'You wrote an email yesterday, the Plant Manager is concerned, and I am concerned with the contents of your email. Where did you find the information you included in the email, the names of the staff, and Oka's case?' she quizzed and carried on. 'We need to understand why you did it.'

I had not copied her in on the email; there was no need to email my queries in a member's capacity. Instead of replying to my email, the Plant Manager, whom I had copied in, had decided to send Vicky to confront me. 'So many people have been forwarded your email. Do you know which people have viewed your email?' She fired a barrage of questions. 'You should have spoken to me before sending a not-well-thought-out letter. I would have answered your questions.'

I replied that I sent the email based on what had been happening in the past ten years; Oka's case had been the spark. I sent the email in my capacity as a member of the fund. I followed the complaint process; all those I copied in were the decision-makers who could make the necessary changes. I needed the benefits list changed and a conversation to begin. All the names I included as references were my colleagues I'd had conversations with before they resigned and left the company. Their plight touched my heart, as had Oka's case now. As a member, I wanted the next person to have access to their contributions to buy their first home without the added pressure and stress of resigning. 'I am happy to meet with directors or anyone who decides on member benefits for the fund. I need the benefits changed as per my email,' I said.

I knew it would not take my email alone to change member benefits, but I did not expect a confrontation between myself and my line manager about the pension fund. A short reply to my email to say the matter will get addressed or reviewed at the following members' annual general meeting would go a long way for any inclusive organisation. Views and opinions vary in how they get expressed; every dissatisfaction aired is a golden opportunity to improve the process or status quo. Learning organisations thrive from complaints; complaints highlight what we think we are doing right but are not. It is diversity in thinking that is more critical than the final construction, the outcome of a process.

After about twenty minutes of explaining my intentions back and forth, I noticed we were not making any progress. Vicky kept mentioning that the Plant Manager was concerned with my email, as was she. *How did they miss the whole doughnut around the hole, focusing just on the hole in the doughnut?* I thought to myself, remembering Napoleon Hill's comments. There was a prolonged silence, my mind racing, past events flashing by, and then I said, 'I feel like I am getting victimised here. If my passion for having the document changed was down here,' I continued, indicating with my arm, 'it's now up here.' I was emotional by then. I excused myself to go to the toilet.

It must have taken forever to come back. I found Vicky still sitting in the same position waiting for me. She said it had not been her intention to victimise me. I could see I wasn't going to concentrate on anything productive that day. I felt sorry for her, and she was a good person carrying out the orders of someone else. She then said, 'Let me hug you before I go.' I didn't see where that came from; it must have been her inner, compassionate self coming out. I stood facing away from her; she walked over to my side and gave me a calming side hug. Compassion and empathy hurt if you are human enough.

And she let go by saying, 'We will get it changed.' Then she left my office.

I packed my laptop into my backpack and lunch box with my morning sandwiches, which I was about to eat when Vicky walked in. Then, backpack in hand, I turned off the lights and closed the self-locking door before walking to the car park. When I got to the car park, I thought of calling Vicky but settled on texting her. I texted her, 'I need time for myself, I can't concentrate, I feel drained.'

She called me an hour later, when I was already home to say I could have as much time as I wanted. She said she understood now how passionate I was about the matter. I guess she had given her feedback to the Plant Manager and Linda, Head of HR. She invited us to have a first home buyer meeting the following Monday at 11 am.

What differentiates us from the other species is an inborn 'self-centralising system' that guides us in our life's paths. We feel it when we have done a good or an evil deed. How you choose to proceed is determined by you, or by your group. An unethical act is not easy to defend in a free society, especially in the workplace. However, the act of questioning and holding ourselves accountable is what develops humanity. When someone forces you to harm another, and you proceed to do it, you will face the jury and judge of your consciousness alone, and you'll accept the guilty verdict, and the sentence on your own. You might get financially rewarded for executing your given tasks, but the universe has a way of taking away what you gain by unethical means. You will receive it with the right hand, and the left hand will give it away, to your disappointment, as it is not yours to keep.

Chapter 19

Sleeping in My Bed

I know you like sleeping in my bed, Son, on your free days from uni, when I am at work. You think it is cosier than your bed, but the mattress comfort is the same as yours as they are the same brand. The only difference is in size.

So, you were surprised to hear me in the lounge at 10:30 am on a Friday when you thought I would be hours away from knocking off. However, I was not surprised to see you curled up in my bed; you still behave the same way you did as a child wanting to sleep in our bed.

You must have noticed something was amiss in your sleepy state as you asked if everything was okay at work. 'All good, Son, go and sleep in your bed,' I had said and I walked back to the lounge.

Nothing should diminish or erode the father-son relationship, from infancy till separation by death. When parents split up and divorce, it is a split between two individuals who were once united by love and marriage. However, the creation or the product (children) should not suffer as much as their parents. Both parents should ensure that no ill-feeling is transferred to their children, as children are innocent, brought into the world by the two individuals. No child causes a parent not to progress, as the parent's choice to breed is their own. Effects need no blame, but the cause deserves blaming for the effects. However, suppose children go through pain and suffering after their parents' divorce. In that case, children should not, as adults, sever their relationship with either of their parents but mend it in the best way possible. The child, when they grow up, should be grateful that they are in the universe due to the two of you.

A seed makes no preference for where it gets planted, and the 'seed' cannot blame the farmer for being sown in infertile soil, for without the farmer, the 'seed' is just a seed in a seed vault. So are we humans before procreation.

There is a lot that we do not know about our existence in this universe. We know the biological creation part, but we do not know for sure what happens after we cease to exist as a physical body. I believe we are three: the body, the mind and the soul. We have the free will to decide, but how different are we from a baobab seedling or an acorn with an established genetic pattern until it becomes a tree? Every individual has their own pattern set; we know we cannot control what has happened, but we can alter or control what is about to happen in the here and now.

Love and respect nullify what occurred in the past, but hate and anger can snowball into the next generation, perpetuating the innocent's suffering. Cherish that parent–child relationship, for your happiness is their happiness. Your sadness is their sadness. No parent rejoices when their offspring suffer, and a parent's unhappiness affects the child. The feeling gets telepathically transferred from one to the other.

I got an inspiring voice message from my dad the following morning after the incident at work. The twelve-hour time difference between your granddad and us has advantages and disadvantages. We wake up to his positive voice messages, the same as my texts. On the other hand, nighttime for us is daytime for him. He would call at midnight in the early days, thinking it was daytime until he adjusted his wall clock to match our time. If he's not sure now, he checks the clock before making a call. His message this morning was to 'remain resolute and not be swayed by negators, for your goal is more important to concentrate on than the negative.'

I had not told him about the incident at work, but his message matched what I needed to hear. Sometimes encouragement comes unsolicited; you only need to say a word, and before you complete a sentence, the listener will have picked a complete picture of what you need. I needed his words more than anything that weekend, which led me to research and read more about how superannuation funds operated; the more I read, the more optimistic I became.

Reading aloud is what I sometimes do as it helps me contextualise and remember essential facts; what I want to recall will end up playing in my head like a song on repeat. My reading is irritating if anyone is in the room, so I do it alone. I know you move to your bedroom when I start reading aloud in the lounge. Thanks for that, Son.

That weekend must have been one of the longest weekends I have ever lived; all I wanted was for the Monday morning meeting to happen. You, however, asked to be dropped off at your mum's house on my way to work. You asked again why I had knocked off early last Friday. Again, I saw the concern in your eyes. 'All is good,' I had said on Friday, which was not the answer you wanted.

What affects us cannot be covered or brushed aside for long. It seeks to be in the open like a seedling breaking out of the soil. I had to tell you. Otherwise, you would have kept worrying about me for the next three days you spent at your mum's house. I told you I had been upset because my company failed to understand the plight of first-home buyers at work. We have a pension fund like KiwiSaver, but it is rigid in that workers have to resign if they want to access their contributions to buy a house.

Remember your first response: 'But we have a first home?'

'Yes, we do have a first home,' I explained. 'It's not about me; it's about my co-workers battling to enter the housing market. House prices have risen to dizzying heights. The needed deposit is challenging to raise. The only option is to seek help from KiwiSaver and superannuation funds. We are having a meeting today to discuss the issue.'

'That's a good cause—I support you. Good luck with your meeting today, Dad.' That's what you said before you got out of the car.

'Thank you, Son,' was my response. I wasn't looking at it as a cause or trying to be a hero like Vicky had said that Friday.

I felt invigorated after dropping you off; you and your granddad had given me the boost I needed. We thrive through encouragement from family and friends, the more that those who are close to us think as we do, the more we achieve what we seek. Behind every medal won in the Olympics is a team supporting the athlete; so are we, in our everyday quests.

Five minutes before the meeting started, I walked into the sales and marketing boardroom, chose the chairperson position and sat waiting for the other three to come. Linda was the first to walk in, warmly greeted me, talked about the weather as we waited for the other two. Finally, Vicky came in at exactly 11 am, explaining that the Plant Manager was not coming. I was a bit disappointed, but not bothered by this.

Linda said the meeting was about the email I had sent last Thursday. 'What is it that drove you to that?' she asked. I repeated my motive and intentions just as I had told Vicky. But I told Linda that I had a house already; it was not about me but about the people who wanted to get into their first home, to which she replied, 'We know you have a house; that's why it is surprising us that you want this changed so much.'

I brought along the member booklet, updated five years prior, and told her that this was the source of all the issues.

It is normal and expected that standards would drop when no questions are asked. What attracts attention is what gets changed.

Linda was professional in her responses, and she had started initiating changes. She said that had I rung her, she would have updated me. She was pleased that my intentions came from a good place and assured me to leave them with her. She needed to contact two more people for the changes; it could take a bit longer, but it would happen.

However, the whole scenario had been a case of negative opinions overriding positive intentions, which often happens when trying to defend a slack we have caused in a process. Defending is the starting process of any war.

Blaming and character assassination comes to the forefront before retraction and evaluating the slack that has been highlighted.

I was happy with Linda's assurances; my email had reached stakeholders who felt the changes were long overdue.

My last statement to Linda was that my email was not about her or Ava, her assistant, but about the document that would outlive us in the company. My intentions were to make it easy for anyone and help our fellow workers get into their first homes. I thanked her, and we all left with broad smiles.

When minds come together to discuss a common issue, you tune in to each other's frequency and self-adjust your thoughts to match the common elements of all involved, and in doing so, come up with a common goal if all desire to have that goal. 'We resonate with your thinking.' That's what Vicky said at the end. It was reassuring that our thinking was in harmony. A collective resonance will always yield a positive outcome for everyone involved.

Compassion, sympathy, empathy, and understanding are some ingredients that are important should you find yourself in a leadership position. Prejudging without the facts laid bare is a sure way of making disastrous decisions, which erode subordinate–leader confidence. As a leader, you need to cultivate that confidence in your subordinates and theirs in you. Do not take a complaint as a challenge to your leadership but embrace the complaint. It allows you to improve things that have been hidden or overlooked. Promptly address the complaint, if possible, or give feedback on progress to the complainant, for it assures and gives confidence that there shouldn't be any fear in raising complaints about the processes.

****

I received a text message from Bria a week after the superannuation meeting asking me to cover for her the following day. Bria was our plant administrator who had joined the organisation the previous year while I was away on my annual leave. She had replaced Emma, who had given short notice and left. The changes had happened quickly, within a couple of weeks. I was surprised to find Emma gone when I returned from my four-week annual leave and was told that she said she had had enough. She had three years of service and got along well with everyone, me included. Emma was a fun lady with a strong French accent. She had once grumbled something about the amount of work and her remuneration being negatively correlated. I advised her to speak to her boss about it. I hadn't asked her how the meeting had gone but assumed the key issues had been amicably addressed.

Even though I was in quality control, I could do some of Bria's tasks and cover for her when she was away.

I replied to Bria's text message that it wasn't an issue. Tuesdays were not as busy for me as Mondays, so not a problem. However, when I contacted her to ask how she was doing, she replied that she was exhausted and had spent the day sobbing in her office.

Work had become overwhelming, and the accounts team was piling work on her even though she was not in the accounts section. I advised her to push back and seek an audience with her boss; this was *déjà vu*. I was repeating what I had urged Emma to do. Bria was in the same situation as Emma.

She texted back that she would have a meeting with her boss and the accounts boss when she returned to work the following Wednesday.

Depending on their employment, people sometimes take on additional work from other departments. Either to learn, impress, or just for its own sake. However, filling in lulls in their usual activities will soon become part of their job. The lack of an additional reward for this becomes a sticky problem when the helpful person gets pressured to meet deadlines that are not technically theirs. When you realise that you have taken more than you can chew, there should be nothing that stops you from saying, 'Hey, team, I think I have more on my plate than I can handle,' without any fear of being reprimanded or labelled as work-shy. Understanding should not be problematic if the task is unassigned to anybody. However, the critical part is that you should complete your essential functions per your contract or agreement. The fear that stops you from raising an overloaded work situation can develop into resentment and dissatisfaction, to which the person responsible for changing your workload is oblivious. Knowing your rights will free you from overloading and locking yourself in the office 'crying'. You should always know that your wellbeing is more important than any additional tasks you add on. No one will feel the pain when your health suffers other than yourself and your family.

When you turn down added tasks, you are not lazy, you are not selfish, neither are you mean, but you are taking care of your mental wellbeing. Organisations have evolved from how they operated a while ago, where profit was more important than worker safety.

Work safety now involves mental health, just as it does the physical aspect. Everyone should go home in the condition they came to work in.

Work stress or burnout can trigger many invisible health issues, unlike a cut to the finger, which is visible until it heals.

> Health issues from stress or burnout:
> – Heart disease, high blood pressure.
> – Can worsen asthma.
> – Obesity, excess fat in the belly.
> – Worsens diabetes in two ways; first, it increases the likelihood of destructive behaviours such as unhealthy eating or excessive drinking; Second, stress seems to directly raise glucose levels of people with type 2 diabetes, according to studies.
> – Headaches—tension, and migraines.
> – Depression and anxiety.
> – Gastrointestinal problems—heartburn and irritable bowel syndrome. It can also worsen ulcers.
> – Accelerated aging.
>
> —umbrella.org.nz, n.d.

How you project yourself is how you end up getting treated in general. No one takes advantage of a knowledgeable person. Your lack of knowledge, and the limitations that you display become your worst nemeses. The knowledge gap can be used against you, which you may unconsciously consent to, though it is against your conscious wish and helplessness to stop it. You give your power away by not knowing what you should be knowing.

When Emma joined the organisation three years before quitting, she needed a job to facilitate her way to a permanent residency visa. Again, she performed above and beyond expectations. However, Emma's salary kept upsetting her every payday. Through frustration, she eventually decided to move on.

On the other hand, Bria got assigned to a function with specified duties but was informed that Emma used to take on additional tasks on top of her role, which were above her pay grade. So, more work kept on being added. Humans have an itch for competing, wanting to be better than the previous. However, sometimes we get to a point where we 'bleed' before we yield.

We have limits and tolerance as humans, and we can only take an extra load for a particular time, provided that what we do is appreciated, acknowledged, and remunerated. The realisation that what we do is beyond what we get paid for creeps in when we stop enjoying the tasks, influenced by the surrounding environment, co-workers, family, friends and media. The treatment you get may or may not be a true reflection of your contribution. Sometimes, a change in mannerisms or behaviour from a boss, teammate, or coworker triggers self-evaluation, leading you to snap or be appreciative. No one knows another's true personality, as you can change and slide from one end of the spectrum to the other without the next person realising.

However, as a leader, you should thank the complainant for raising the issue and encourage them to report any problems should they come across more.

Learning as individuals should not stop when we leave school, college or university. The process should be ongoing as the world does not stop progressing when we get our qualifications.

Technology will constantly evolve. Learning is not only sitting in class; anything that gives a fresh perspective on our thinking is learning. The process can also apply to organisations; education should not stop or be limited to a select few because of competing priorities. Everyone should be on the same page for the organisation to be fluid in its operational activities.

Strive to make yourself available for any training you receive and suggest training programmes to the facilitator that will benefit you, your co-workers and the organisation. Most organisations have a training budget set aside, which works well with a dedicated person for training programmes. As a leader, you have a strong business case to resuscitate training programmes if there is a provision for a training budget. As a worker, you also have a solid chance to help restore training programmes; a worker who wants to learn has productivity at heart.

Chapter 20

Your Path

We choose what we want to become and work towards that desire. Getting to the desired goal may be out of our control, but focus, determination and passion can remain in our possession. Those who will aid you will be in place strategically along your path; once you reach that point, the aider will move you to your next station, where another will be waiting. We are all connected and are playing our helping role in exchange for the help we need. We only get the support we need to achieve our goals by helping others. When you stop the conveyor-belt of assisting others, for selfish reasons, your needed help will also stop coming your way, and progress towards what you desire will stall.

In families, workplaces, churches, businesses or politics, the path remains unchanged in supporting others. Your help to others is their help, and their help is your help. Those who require your helping hand will come for your help differently; the quicker you identify them, the faster you progress toward your own goals.

Selective helping is as bad as not helping. Beyond what we see is something that does not have physical form. When you help someone, you are helping the entity housed in that body, which resembles none of what you see. You are helping what they are inside, the same as you are inside. That is beyond what you see and touch.

When you receive your wishes and desires, it is a recognition and a reward for your good deeds. The one who judges your progress and allows you to succeed is the one who has acknowledged your help, the one to whom you have given genuine assistance with no expectations in return. If someone asks for your support, it is not an invitation to take advantage of that individual, community or country. There is a separation between doing business and assisting. No individual, community or nation wants to have a begging bowl in front of them, but unfortunate circumstances would have led them to be where they are. Suppose you were to look genuinely deeper into the past of that person, community or country. In that case, one will find many causes, and preceding events. Some effects take generations to show in a population. Other outcomes are instant; regardless of how they got into their situation when help was needed, you help and do so without seeking attention or recognition for yourself.

When you desire attention and praise, it ceases to be beneficial and is more about highlighting your privileged position. Would you want to be paraded around as the unfortunate one if the tables turned? I doubt it. The universe can recognise the genuineness of your helping hand and thus, reward you or take away part of what you must compensate the unfortunate ones until you become genuine in your helping.

When you take the approach that the needy are you in them and you are all from the same source, their smiling or sad face is your face. You are one, only separated by wealth, which you cannot take with you to your next life and thus can share and make them smile as you do. Fortunes are easily reversible.

I got a text message from an old friend. It had been a couple of months since we had communicated, on her son's birthday, to be precise. She and her husband had invited me to their son's birthday party, which I failed to attend due to other commitments, but I sent my wishes.

A few years back, I had helped them financially when one of their family members had a medical emergency overseas. I had money aside that I could spare.

They now wanted to borrow some money and needed it urgently; I was their last hope, so she said. I asked how much they needed, and she said five to six thousand in the next couple of days; this was Saturday, and Monday would be the day they needed the money. I couldn't make an instant decision. I said I would get back to her after checking my finances.

Only lend money to someone when you are willing to never receive it back, with no resentment on your part and no expectations about repayment dates, even if they promise them. The relationship is more important than the money owed.

After I had checked my financial fitness, I could not lend my friends the requested amount. I got back to them and told them that it was unfortunate that I could not help them and wished them luck. When you want to help, but you can't or it would cause you to make sacrifices that you would regret, stop the helping or assistance, as you may end up with unwanted emotional baggage that can turn your progress backward.

When you cannot help someone after they seek your assistance, you are not the right person to assist that person now. Someone else will be placed along that person's route with the resources and flexibility to help them. All that person needs to do is seek divine intervention, be persistent, and eventually they will be directed to a source that can provide them with what they need. In seeking assistance, you do not need to be resentful after getting an unfavourable answer, but should bless and thank the person who has not been able to help. When you become resentful, the waiting period to get your desires is prolonged.

***

Your life's path is shaped by how you incorporate what you possess through heredity, education and your environment, which you then transform to create the course you want through your mind. You have the capabilities to create what you so desire to the standards you set.

Creating anything you want is no different from starting a family when you get to the age you want to start your family. You will think of falling in love first, and then you will seek the girl of your desire with the features and personality you have in your mind. After that, you create the connection through any mutual means—face-to-face talk, phone, social media, etcetera.

Being in love is more about the brain than the heart, though culture and media point to the heart as the source of love. We see images of the cupid's arrow on Valentine's Day messages, aimed at the heart, not the brain, so many of us then believe it is all in the heart, but alas, no, it is the brain. The limbic system is part of the brain involved in our behavioural and emotional responses, part of which is geared towards reproduction, and caring plays that critical part.

All the emotions and how instantly we fall in love come from that limbic system. The increase in blood flow, the feel-good chemicals that set off emotional turmoil, affection, lust, attraction, contentment, happiness, curiosity, attachment and fear of rejection are some of the emotions that come from your brain. However, *you* have control.

Nevertheless, those emotions will manifest into physical reactions, such as your heart racing, increased energy, increased breathing, sleeplessness, flushed cheeks and hormonal changes.

After you find that person, you create a relationship leading to marriage, or the ideal relationship you have envisioned. You will then have the number of children you want to procreate in your mind, verbalise your family size with your partner, and then work on achieving that size target. All are visualisations from your mind. Regardless of how you go about it, the trigger will have come from your mind to do what you do.

Any accomplishment you achieve, positive or negative, follows the same principle as starting a family. The path to your goal can be long and windy. However, what is essential is to focus your mind on the target and not lose sight of your next step. You may fail many times, but it is crucial to take the learnings from your failings, correct your plans, implement them, and move closer to the goal until you reach it.

Remember, Son, all your creations are held in your mind only to come to fruition when a burning desire has overcome limitations, self-set or set by others for you. So is the universe we live in, which is held in the mind of All, The Source, God, or any name you choose. He then creates physical beings when the time is right, unlike humans who get bogged down by the lack and limitations we set in our minds alongside our creations.

We are creators like God, but our results are finite, unlike God's infinite creations. We cannot claim to be God, but we can claim that we are created in his image and have some abilities to create what we want. Our creations mirror some of his creations but only at a lower level, for he is the one who inspires us to transform our thoughts into reality when we seek his intervention through the many ways at our disposal.

If you ask me how we got to be walking the path we are on now, from a spiritual perspective, I would say we chose our route while in another state, way before we entered our human bodies. If we believe in a life after life, there should be a belief in life before life. Our parents got used as the conduits of our entry points into this world. Your mother and I wanted a child, like any other parents, and you chose to be with us, to walk life's journey as our physical child as we chose to be your biological parents. You chose to seek our guidance as we chose to guide you. We humans comprise the body, mind and spirit. All living beings are that way, plants included.

We are similar in some ways to cars, spacecraft, or any other mechanical machine that uses some form of energy to move from one point to the next. What differentiates us from machines, however, is the spirit. The devices, like ourselves, have a physical body designed, shaped and built in the same way. Like human brains, they contain an engine or central processing unit, a computer, that guides and offers instructions on the best course of action. The machines need a source of power to get going, which comes in the form of petrol, diesel, electricity, solar and so on; humans need food. However, we have a spirit that, when it exits our bodies, is the end of physical living; the physical body dies, and memories get erased with that departure.

In contrast, when a car or machine gets destroyed beyond repair, a mould creates another with the same properties as the last one, and memory is transferable into the new engine.

Creating a human with the same experiences as the dead does not happen as in machines. The spirit does not die; neither does it hold earthly memories as they get stored in the brain, which fails with the body.

We entered our mothers' wombs to complete the creation as a physical body from the spirit world. The matter is energy, so you become the energy in the 'matter', the baby. According to the law of conservation of energy, energy can neither be created nor destroyed. But it can be transformed from one state of energy to another. Therefore the 'energy' you were in the spirit world knew its preferences before transforming into the person you are or the person I am. Meaning that we get directed to the path we walk now or choose it ourselves to fulfil a purpose or a calling.

We walk to our calling, we walk to our objective, and we walk to our goals. The lane we walk in this life's journey is what we asked for in the past. It is the actions of the past that manifest today. To change tomorrow's outcome, we must adjust today's trajectory. There is no such thing as achieving goals or objectives without putting in some effort. Obstacles you face and overcome are the price you pay for your wishes. The obstacles become the way. There is a correspondence between what you are expending and your desired outcome. So, be prepared for obstacles along the way to your goals. You will face them, and how you displace them determines the new obstacles along the path as you edge closer to the destination.

Getting to your goal by any means does not mean abusing and taking away the rights of other human beings but working together for a common purpose. Remember that there are many goals tied to your goal. Therefore, the success of your plan is the success of your helpers' goals too.

Every journey you take is a significant journey, and every trip you do not accept is still essential, as no one walks your journey but yourself. We take 'journeys' to discover what we perceive as missing, in search of life's fulfilment, or to escape physical discomfort. We take 'journeys' to taste happiness. We take 'journeys' to bring comfort to our loved ones. Every journey leads to another, as we discover the next bit that completes the puzzle.

We give up on our journeys daily, retreat, refill, take up the quest the following day, achieve and travel again. We then completely give up on our trips when we have allowed the matter between our ears to be as barren as the Sahara Desert, as we see it, but it is only to you and me, as deep down in its belly it holds enough water for it to be productive again. So, you pivot, refocus, and out comes the energy to move again and flourish like the trees of Lebanon.

Exposure gives a broader perspective, thickens lenses, opens horizons, and we approach any task from a good vantage point, turning challenges into conquests. My journeys to these various organisations exposed me to review my past experiences. You can only describe bitterness in fruit if you have tasted a sweet one; you can only describe how sweet a lollipop is if you have tasted a bitter one. Without comparisons, our attempt to pass judgment is futile.

However, a good deed in Antarctica is a good deed in the Kalahari. A good deed in Vanuatu is a good deed in Venezuela. Equally, an evil act in the Kalahari is also evil in Antarctica; an evil deed in Venezuela is equally evil in Vanuatu. We do not need to cross the globe to verify our assumptions, as these are inborn and brought out by intuition. The virtuous and vicious acts cross cultures, languages, ethnicities and country boundaries. Justification of either action is not necessary or required. The receiver of the deed would have made their judgment upon receiving it.

I had been out on a mission to verify my assumptions over some deeds; one part of the findings was myself. Often, we tend to look outward and try to find the causes of our circumstances, and we sanitise or minimise the part that we have played.

The families we come from, the communities we grew up in, and the elements that fostered recognition and respect within our societies cling to and direct our responses to the challenges we face in the open world on our paths to our goals. What we 'resolved', how we 'resolved' it, when and why we 'resolved' it, and who accepted the resolution, might be like new challenges but infinitely different. Any attempt to apply past solutions to a present snag can yield frustration at the least and disaster at the worst. However, learning to unlearn some of what got engraved and encrypted in our core values, beliefs and thinking system frees us from holding ourselves back.

We become stubborn against change if the change is forced on us. Stubbornness and self-resistance, however, might lead to a lack of progress. Reassessing your strategy and staying in rhythm with the current flow is the only way to calm the situation. If you do not oppose the flow, it will not spit you out or leave you behind. Flow with the tide while mastering your moves, and then step aside when you are confident your new ways will yield the desired results.

Blaming others is a way of comforting yourself and maintaining your ego temporarily. We can blame others as much as we want, but that will not give us long-term results, if any, if the source of our misfortunes is ourselves.

Knowledge can be power, but it is only power when you know how to use it. You can control most of what happens in your life. You choose and select your helpers through your goal setting. You will consistently achieve when you have a strong will, desire and passion for any goal you set your mind on. The only thing that can stop the desired outcome is yourself.

When you want to go east, west, north or south, you need to know directions, but having none cannot stop you either; all that information does not need to be in you. What you need to possess is the knowledge of where and how to get that information. The knowledge that guides you to the right place, the right people and the right direction is that power part: that which harnesses all that you require to transmute your dreams into tangibles that you can touch and be proud of is the power. However, knowledge acquired and unused is as good as money hidden in the basement. Knowledge is supposed to work for you, the possessor, but not against you; unused, it becomes useless and redundant.

****

I moved from one company factory to another doing side jobs; I would take time to reflect during my smoko breaks on the whole purpose of my being where I was. There was a little bit of extra money going into my bank account, but my main objective was to get exposed to other work settings and different work cultures. I came to a new country and culture and had some uncomfortable work experiences. How I could have answered a work experience question would have been very skewed. How I could have advised someone based on the organisation I worked for could have been inaccurate.

The organisations I worked for ranged from having fifty to 2500 employees on the same premises. What became apparent was that the more prominent the organisation was, the more politically correct it was. The smaller the organisation, the smaller the focus on political correctness. The larger the organisation, the more diversified it was, which meant the views and opinions of those who drove the organisation's culture were more open and varied. The core of most businesses is their employees; however, the person or persons at the top set the bar for the organisation. The checks, monitoring, and measures will distinguish what the organisation stands for. Smaller organisations with fifty or fewer employees have a more vital connectedness than larger ones. However, at times profits and set targets will override and overlook some core guiding principles of the companies.

Who constitutes the leadership team tends to affect the overall political correctness of the smaller companies as they lack the diversity of larger organisations.

If you are deciding which organisation size to join, the perfect fit matters. Some small organisations are best to work for as they have family togetherness as a core principle, so every employee joining the organisation becomes a family member. They want the best for their employees at work and away from work.

Larger organisations can also offer the best of what you want. There are opportunities for growth and development. However, on a negative note, covertly and veiled in ethnicity, some job opportunities may align more with some groups when they arise. If you feel disadvantaged and complain, you can still expect an immediate response to your concerns since standards and accountability are high on their priority list.

It is worth researching the company or organisation before you decide to join. Information can be found on the company or organisation's website, in the local press, and on the web through a search engine. Knowing someone already employed in the company or organisation will be an added advantage, as the person can provide you with unfiltered information. Above all, knowing your rights, your worth and what you want to achieve should you join the organisation is as essential as joining the right organisation. If you do not have growth plans, you may remain stagnant.

Additionally, suppose you choose to be a business owner. In that case, you synthesise information from organisations and individuals to develop the most suitable solution that works to your benefit and for all stakeholders.

The story of Rocket Lab exemplifies this; Peter Beck, the developer, knew what he desired from an early age and refused to let setbacks and discouragement deter him or his parents from pursuing his dreams.

His parents got told by his high school career counsellor that his career aspirations did not fit any 'pre-defined boxes' and were 'absurdly unachievable'.

He overcame wet blankets who discouraged others from embarking on their visions. These people are everywhere, in families, workplaces and even churches. He did not follow the usually prescribed route of the university and mastering a discipline before spacecraft engineering. His path was already existing and natural in his mind's eye. He attracted the players, enablers, and the whole cast to achieve his dream with his vision, passion and desire.

Changing jobs, moving from one organisation to the next in search of the best fit before self-reflection and self-correcting can be a case of chasing your tail. The same issues will replicate and follow you wherever you move, and thus you might think that the world is against you because of who you are.

Changing your thinking pattern or frequency will be the way to move away from what you don't want. Letting go of the negative loads you harbour, resentment, anger and frustration, will make you likeable. The negative 'load' broadcasts itself wherever you go. It is displayed and transmitted as you interact with others. As human beings, our connectivity is like a circuit node that makes others tune into our aura, picking the negative or positive feelings and reciprocating accordingly. Changing your thought pattern to the positive alters the situation altogether, making you lighter for others to 'lift'.

When we give obstacles and hindrances attention, they control us, worsening whatever we are going through. To change your world, you need to change your vibration; it cleans your thought pattern of all negatives, fear, doubt, despair, apprehension, anger, resentment and frustration, and replaces them with faith.

You have had good things happen in your life; good things are what you need; good things will come again. What God has done before, God will do again. Your faith can have God 'restore to you the years that the swarming locust has eaten, the crawling locust, the consuming locust, and the chewing locust, my great army which I sent among you' (Joel 2:25, New King James Version). Your renewed thinking will provide you with all your wants.

You cannot change the world for yourself, but you can change for the world. God granted us the ability to select what, who, when, where and how to transform our lives. These must be expressed, used and aligned with common causes and beliefs.

By changing your inner world, you change your outer world.

How you view the world will change as your perspective changes. Most of us follow the laid-down pattern, a controlled pattern controlled by a few. Only some people can be in the controlling few. However, anyone can handle whatever they want, thus deviating from the common controlled cause while still remaining within the grounds to develop a new cause in themselves, eventually becoming a cause for all.

It takes creativity, imagination and intuition driven by a strong will and desire to transfer a cause in your mind into a cause for all, unifying the free choices of individuals into a collective will.

As we journey through this plane of life, we collect emotional and physical experiences. Good and bad, positive, and negative. We turn those experiences into what we can use as reference points when we face similar circumstances as individuals. Also, we pass them on as a reference for those that we are bound to help and guide. It takes less time to resolve challenges. Progress becomes swift, hence the reason I am sharing my story with you. Should you require guidance, remember the stories I've told you over the weekend and at other times.

It would be best to remember, Son, that you are in this beautiful country right now because I created this experience in my mind long before you were born; some parts of the puzzle fit nicely in place, but some pieces fell off and got lost. I am still searching for lost details and the picture is visible. I have the option of realigning and rearranging it on this board or changing it altogether.

I touch what I see and feel because I thought about what I wanted to see and touch long before it became a reality. I will use the experience to recreate and realign my plans the way I did before. The principle of planning and executing is the same, only refined, and polished if done for the second, third or fourth time.

****

We were both fatigued but full of thoughts from our conversation as the sun set at the end of a long weekend. I had repeated some points these last two days, so I summarised what I wanted to say to Junior the most.

Junior had sat on the chaise longue listening attentively like a neophyte in a monastery, letting me talk most of the time only breaking in if he needed clarification or to make a comment.

Remember this, Son, I said. Every one of us in this universe is an extension of the All. The only thing that divides us, the human species, is ignorance passed down generations through heredity, environment and education.

As you journey through this plane of the universe, do not be deceived by those trying to split humanity based on a divisive perception of who we are as a human race. We are one, and one of your objectives is to treat the next person like yourself. What harms them harms you. Living in that frame of thinking attracts other beings who think as you do, thereby contributing to a healthy society devoid of divisions, hatred and separation. Your plans will be incorporated with enablers who share similar beliefs to yours.

As much as I wanted to find the differences in the core values of organisations l worked for, perception separated each one from the other on my part. At the core of every business is its workers. There might be a disjuncture in how some companies value the workers and how the workers view the business. Still, the differences become null and void for the entity to function and progress. How you rate one business against another is subjective and relative to your judgment, based on some experiences or collected information.

Subjectivity is how you view a situation from your perspective. Your perspective follows your thinking pattern so that you view situations the way you want.

Organisations are a collection of individuals, and individuals can misstep and toe-step others where control checks are obscure. These isolated cases can cloud good judgment where judgment is required. These few individuals with inflated egos can ruin the reputation of good organisations.

First impressions last, where first impressions turn out to be false impressions, the misalignment between actual reality and alternative reality can be hard to reconcile for either party, becoming a frustrating spiral and leading to resentment.

Where frustration persists and your ability to change the situation is limited, reduce further self-damage by altering your expectations while reconfiguring and redirecting your energy to find better options that can provide achievable outcomes. Frustration and failure are signs of a success not reached, and it will only be reachable when a change in the status quo occurs.

When you know you have the power to influence the outcomes of your situation, you will not have any hatred, friction or resentment toward any human being. The 'power' is in you.

One enemy within you can be your ego. The ego, like everything else, has duality—the negative and the positive. The negative ego can cause havoc if obeyed and left unchecked. This negative ego can keep you trapped in your past like a kingpin in a river, bringing out all injustices, old hurts, perceived mistakes, and everything else of no current significant importance.

Change happens when you recognise that you can make mistakes and learn more from listening to others, not your voice. The recognition, therefore, orders the negative ego to disappear. Whether accepting help and assistance from others or receiving and taking correct measures, your dignity will remain intact. You can be respected by apologising. You are not rich in everything; humility does not mean being weak.

Whatever you can make, so can the other person. Before you get harsh on others, take a moment of reflection. You will find that person is no worse than you. We hate in others what we hate in ourselves. Self-correcting what you hate in yourself leaves you with no hate for the other person.

Regardless of any religion you choose to follow, what is critical is knowing how to self-correct for society's benefit and for your own. Only you can walk your path, I concluded.

I will remember this weekend, Dad. I now have a story I can pass on to your grandkids, Junior said.

We both felt a sense of accomplishment and satisfaction as we stood and walked to the kitchen to make dinner.

Bibliography

Here are some books and other resources that have informed the ideas in the preceding pages...

Marcus Aurelius. *Meditations*. New York: Quarto, 2021.

Richard Bach. *Jonathan Livingstone Seagull: a story*. Dublin: HarperCollins, 2014.

Dale Carnegie. *The quick and easy way to effective speaking*. Mumbai: Wilco, 2017.

Dale Carnegie. *How to develop self-confidence and influence people by public speaking*. Mumbai: Wilco, 2019.

Ariana Eunjung Cha. 'Sleep study on modern-day hunter-gatherers dispels notion that we're wired to need 8 hours a day'. *Washington Post*. 2015. www.washingtonpost.com/news/to-your-health/wp/2015/10/16/sleep-study-on-modern-day-hunter-gatherers-dispels-notion-that-were-wired-to-need-8-hours-a-day/.

David Chester. 'Sadism and aggressive behaviour: Inflicting pain to feel pleasure'. *Personality and Social Psychology Bulletin*. 2018. doi.org/10.1177/01461672188163.

Paulo Coelho. *The Alchemist*. London: Thorsons, 1995.

Marsilio Ficini. 'Liber III', *The Letters of Marsilio Ficino*. London: Shepheard Walwyn Publishers, 1978.

Neville Goddard. 'Feeling Is the Secret'. YouTube: Master Key Society, 2021.

Goldberg Jones. 'Divorce statistics: From the interesting to the surprising.' 2021. www.goldbergjones-or.com/divorce/interesting-divorce-statistics/

Thich Nhat Hanh. *Present Moment Wonderful Moment*. Great Britain: Penguin, 2021.

Thich Nhat Hanh. *The Art of Communicating*. Great Britain: Penguin, 2021.

Thich Nhat Hanh. *At Home in the World*. Great Britain: Penguin, 2022.

Thich Nhat Hanh. *How to Focus*. Dublin: Penguin, 2022.

Louise Hay. 'You can heal your life'. YouTube audio book: Mindset for Success. 2022.

A. Heeren, et al. 'Assessing public speaking fear with the short form of the Personal Report of Confidence as a Speaker scale: confirmatory factor analyses among a French-speaking community'. *Neuropsychiatric Disease and Treatment*, Volume 9, 609–618, 2013. doi.org/10.2147/NDT.S43097

Napoleon Hill. *Think and Grow Rich*. Capstone, 2009.

Robert Kiyosaki. *Rich Dad Poor Dad*. United States: Plata, 2022.

New Zealand Government. *Employment Relations Act 2000*. www.legislation.govt.nz/act/public/2000/0024/latest/DLM58317.html#DLM60340

New Zealand Government. *Human Rights Act 1993*. www.legislation.govt.nz/act/public/1993/0082/latest/whole.html

James Patterson. *The Stories of My Life*. Australia: Penguin, 2022.

Jordan Peterson. *12 Rules for Life: An antidote to chaos*. Australia: Penguin, 2018.

Jordan Peterson. *Beyond Order: 12 more rules for life*. Australia: Penguin, 2021.

_____. 'Pre-industrial societies'. *Current Biology* 25, 2862–2868. doi.org/10.1016/j.cub.2015.09.046

Rasmussen, et al. 'Meta-analytic connections between forgiveness and health'. *Psychology and Health*, 2019. doi.org/10.1080/08870446.2018.1545906.

Dr Robert Russel. *You Can Get What You Want*. United States: Audio Enlightenment Press, 2022.

Jonathan Sacks. *The Power of Ideas*. Australia: Hachette, 2022.

Florence Scovel Shinn. 'The power of the spoken word'. YouTube audio book: Nevillution, 2021.

Florence Scovel Shinn. 'The secret door to success'. YouTube audio book: Nevillution, 2021.

Florence Scovel Shinn. 'The game of life and how to play it'. YouTube audio book: Master Key Society, 2022.

Florence Scovel Shinn. 'Your word is your ward'. YouTube audio book: Nevillution, 2022.

Peter Senge. *The Fifth Discipline: The art and practice of the learning organisation*. London: Crown Business, Random House, 1990.

Robin Sharma. *The Everyday Hero*. Australia: HarperCollins, 2021.

Statista. 'Median duration of marriages and civil unions ending in divorce in New Zealand from 1996 to 2018'. 2023. www.statista.com/statistics/1081514/new-zealand-marriage-and-civil-union-duration/

Eckhart Tolle. *A New Earth: Awakening to your life's purpose*. United States: Penguin, 2005.

Eckhart Tolle. *The Power of Now*. San Francisco: New World Library, Namaste, 2018.

G. Yetish, et al. 'Natural sleep and its seasonal variations in three Pre-Industrial societies'. Cell Press, 2015.

www.ingramcontent.com/pod-product-compliance
Lightning Source LLC
Chambersburg PA
CBHW051421290426
44109CB00016B/1389